The Ar

John Tenniel

Through the Looking-Glass and What Alice Found There

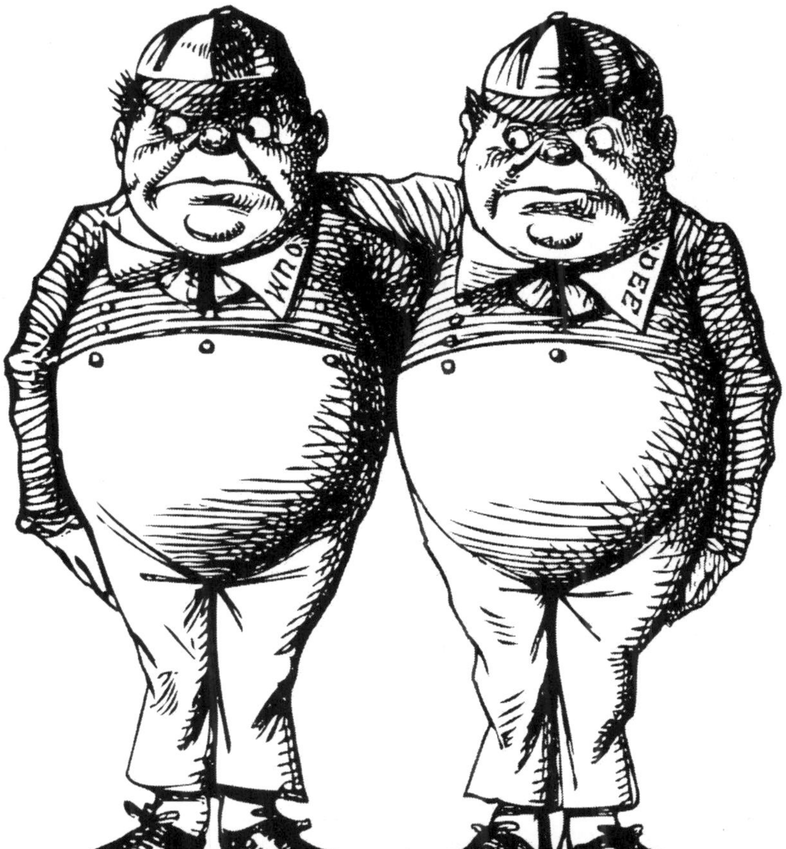

A Vintage Coloring Book

www.vintagecoloring.com

ISBN: 978-1-941766-11-8

Cover image colored with the following Crayola colored pencils: navy blue, light blue, cerulean, black, orchid, pale rose, raspberry, orange, yellow orange, violet, slate, mango, harvest gold, dark brown, brown, light brown, gray, taupe, tan, sand, pine green, green, jade, yellow green, peach, and salmon.

Bibliographical Note: These images, while in the public domain, have been digitally processed and manually cleaned specifically for this collection from scans of the original printed pages. Their intent is for personal use only or for the purpose of review. Please send any questions via the contact form on www.vintagecoloring.com.

The following is a complete collection of the fifty illustrations John Tenniel (1820-1914) created for Through the Looking-Glass and What Alice Found There, the sequel to Alice's Adventures in Wonderland, written by Lewis Carroll. Alice returns, along with the Mad Hatter (in and out of chains). Well-known characters such as Humpty Dumpty, Tweedledum and Tweedledee, the Jabberwock, and the Walrus and the Carpenter, are joined by the White Knight, the Red and White Queens, and the Knitting Sheep, among others. The artwork is ordered the same as it appeared in the novel.

In order to preserve the original proportions of the illustrations, some are presented in a landscape format, while most are portrait orientation. All images are printed single-sided.

The last few pages are intentionally left blank so you have a place to try out the coloring implements of your choice.

Due to the thickness of the paper, colored pencils are recommended. Markers may be used, though having a sheet of cardstock or a few pieces of copy paper under the page you are coloring is useful to prevent possible bleed-through onto the next illustration.

Thank you for your patronage. I hope you enjoy this vintage coloring book, no matter what your age.

Heidi Berthiaume, Curator Prime
www.VintageColoring.com

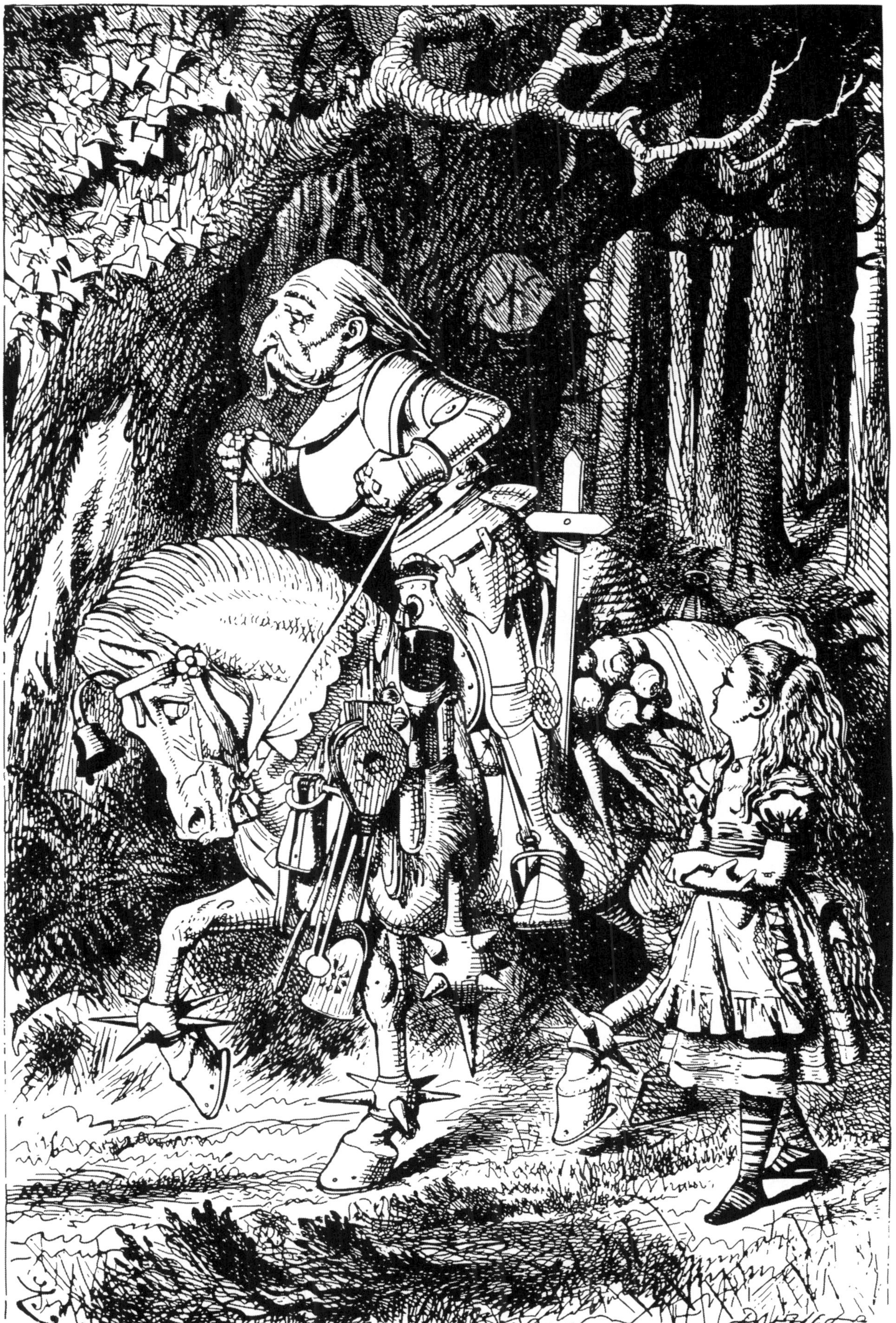

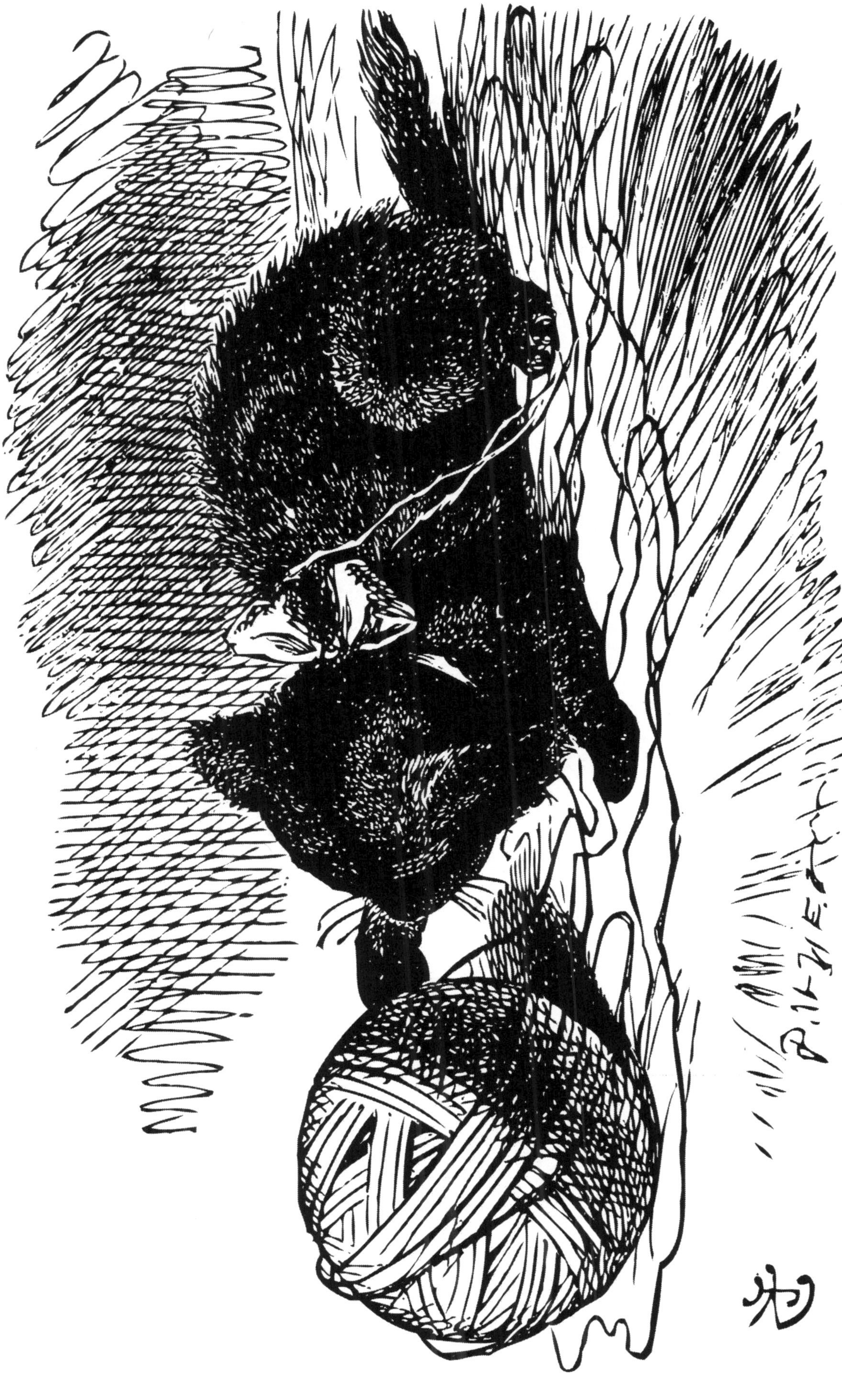

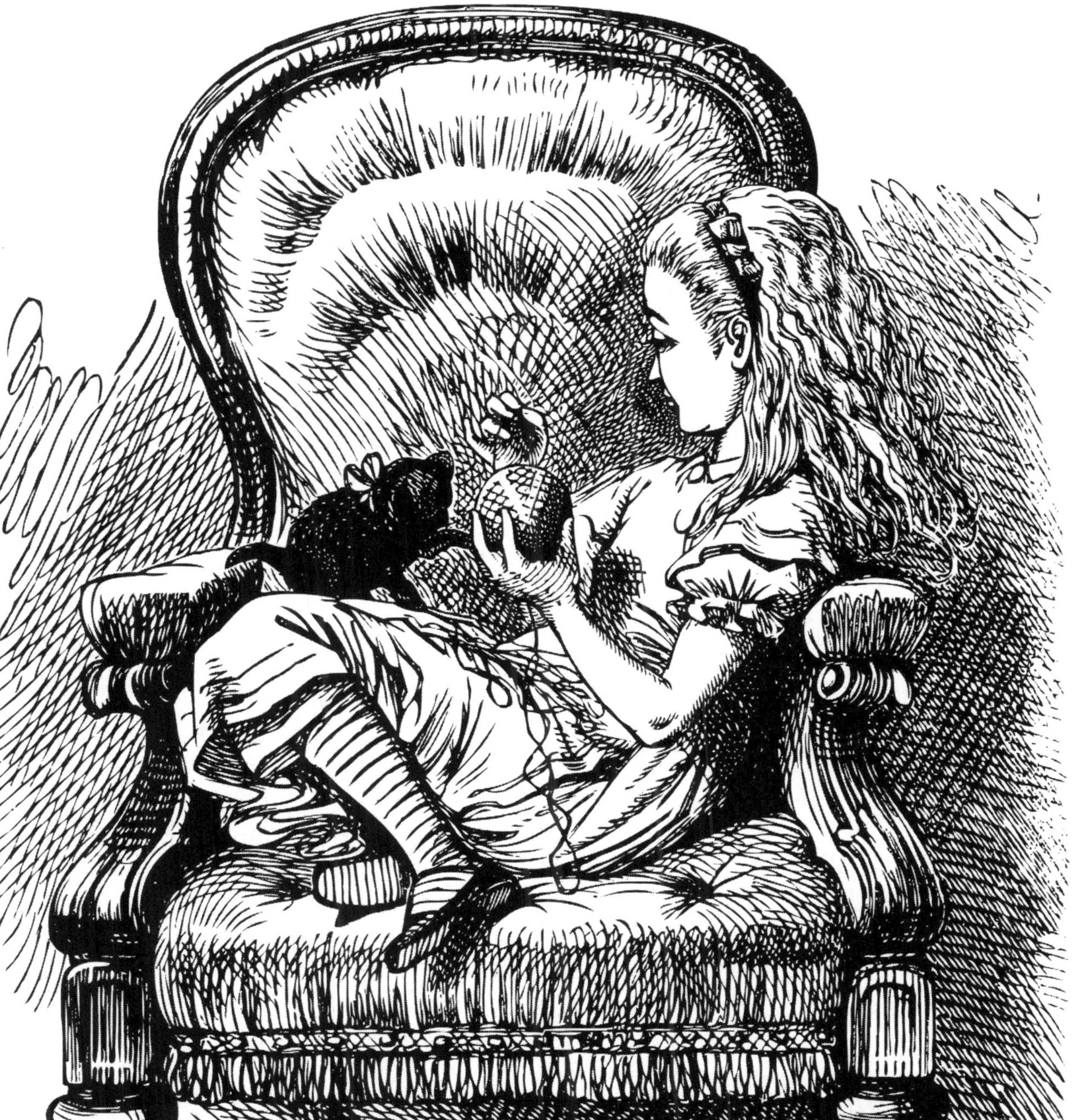

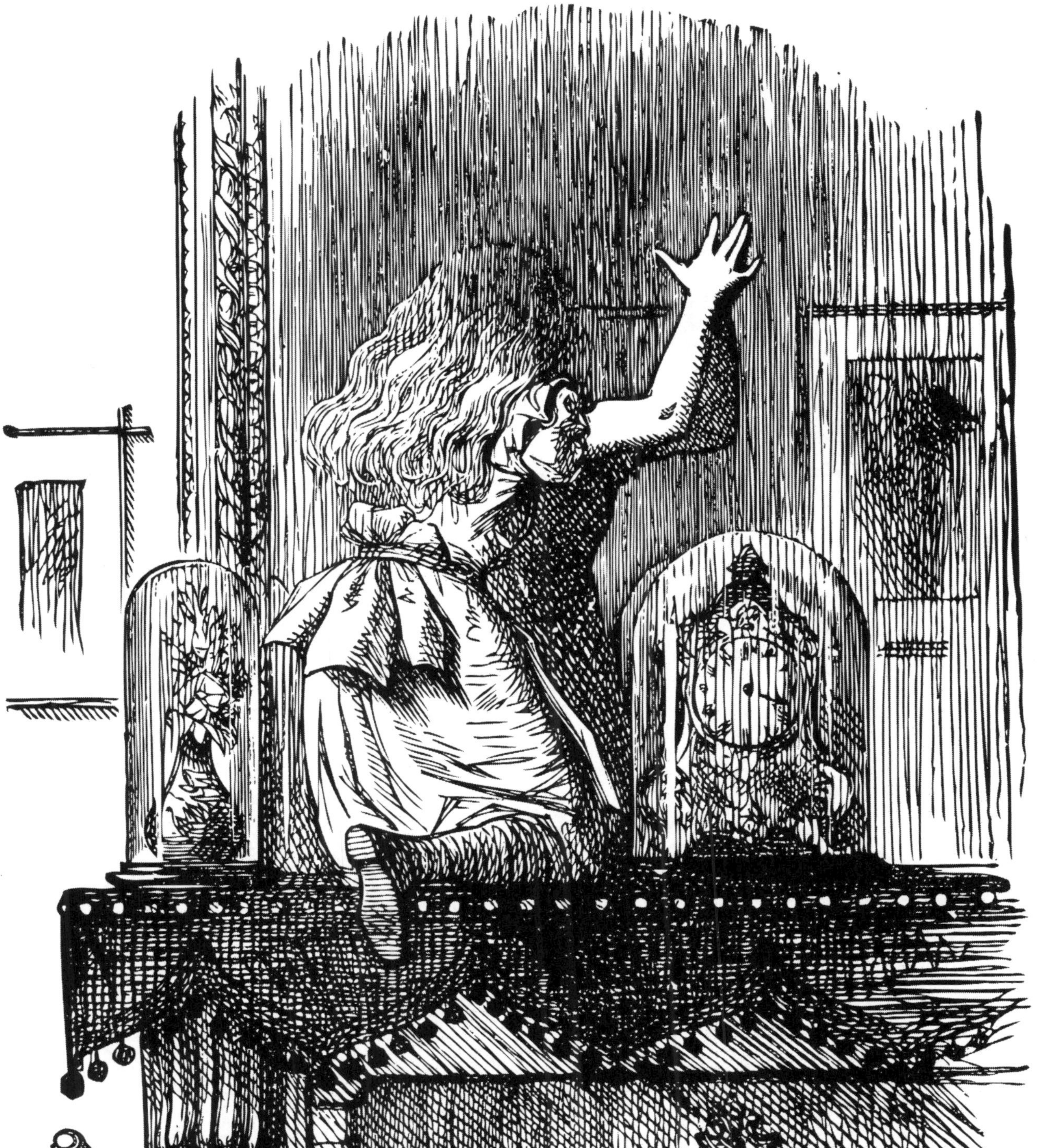

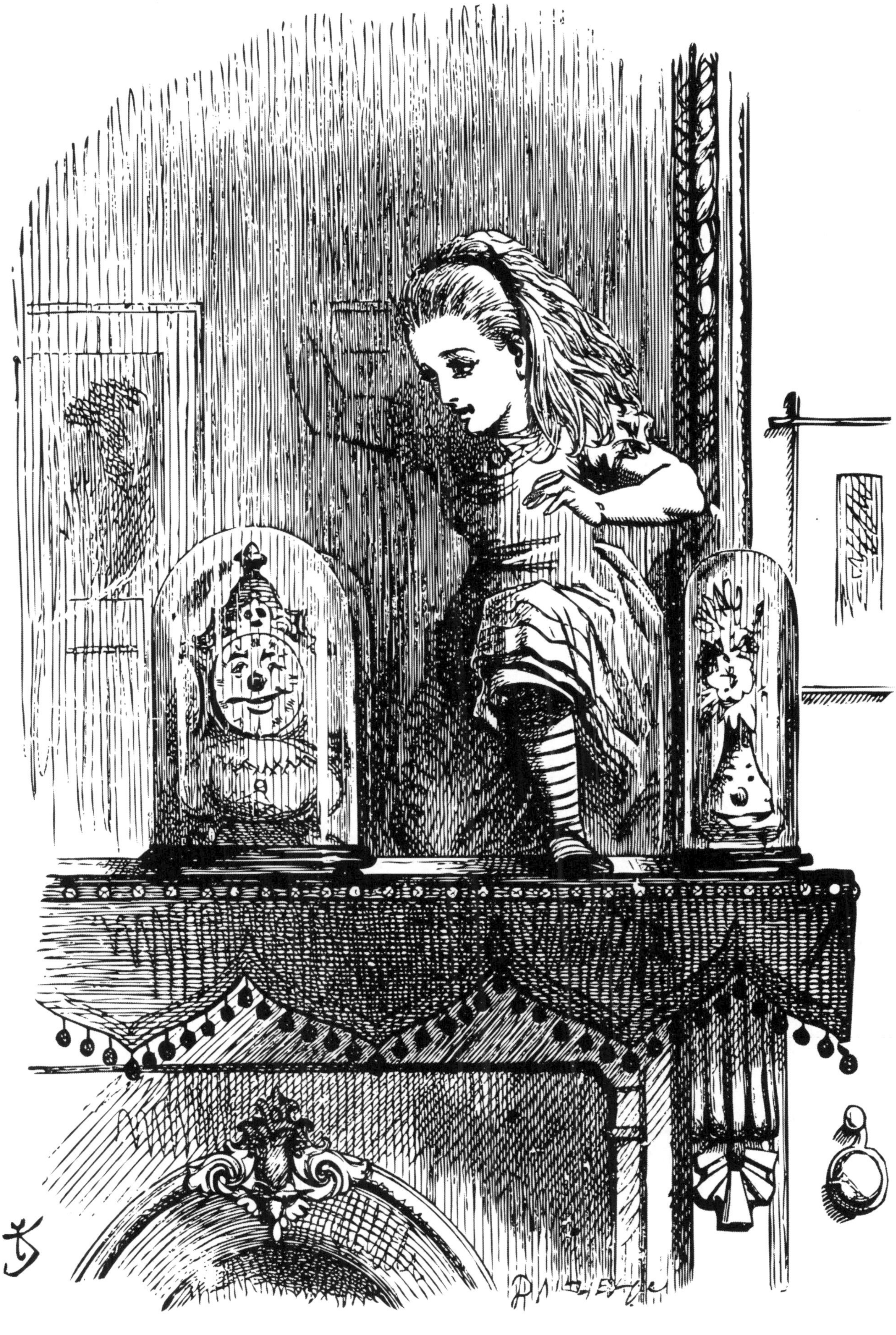

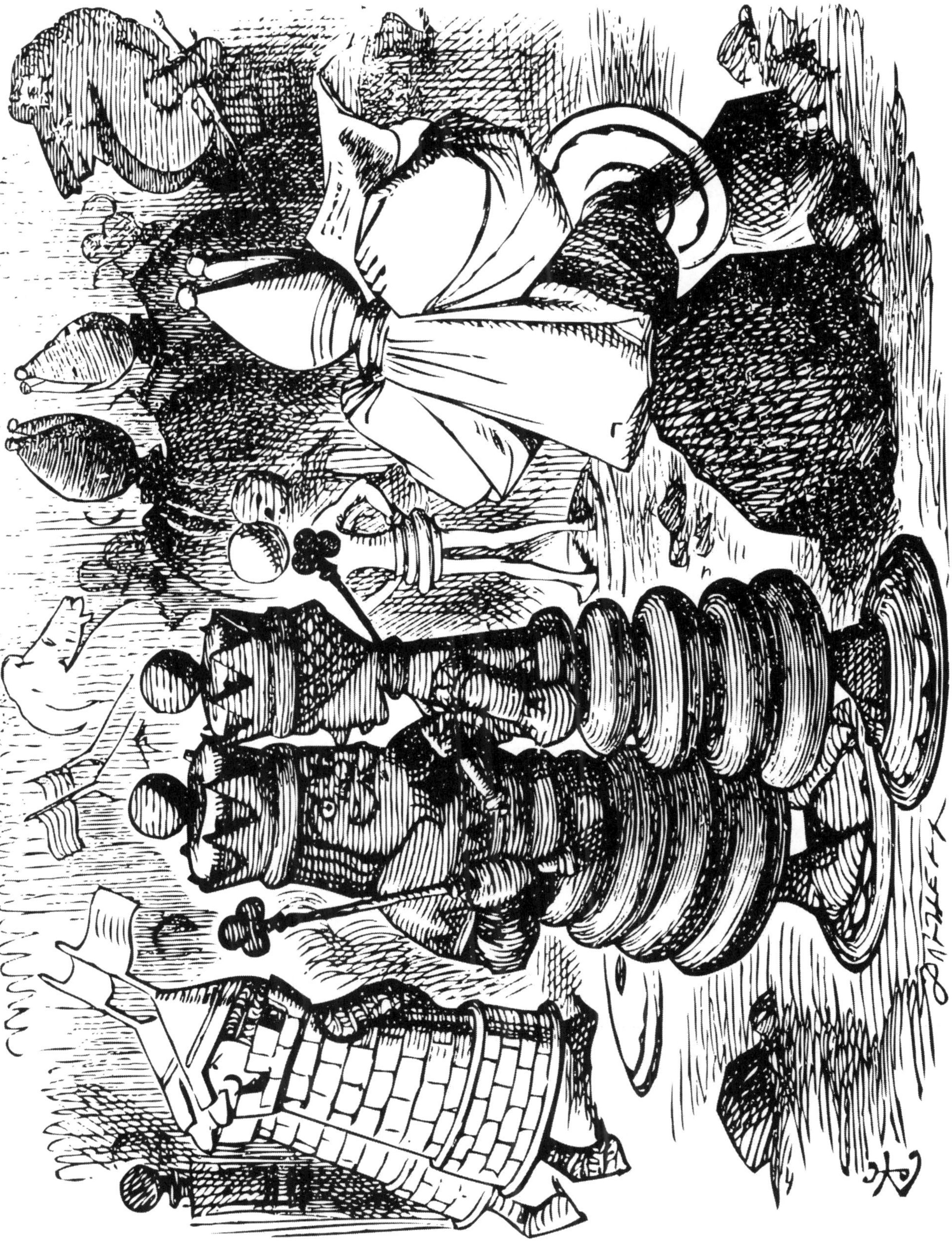

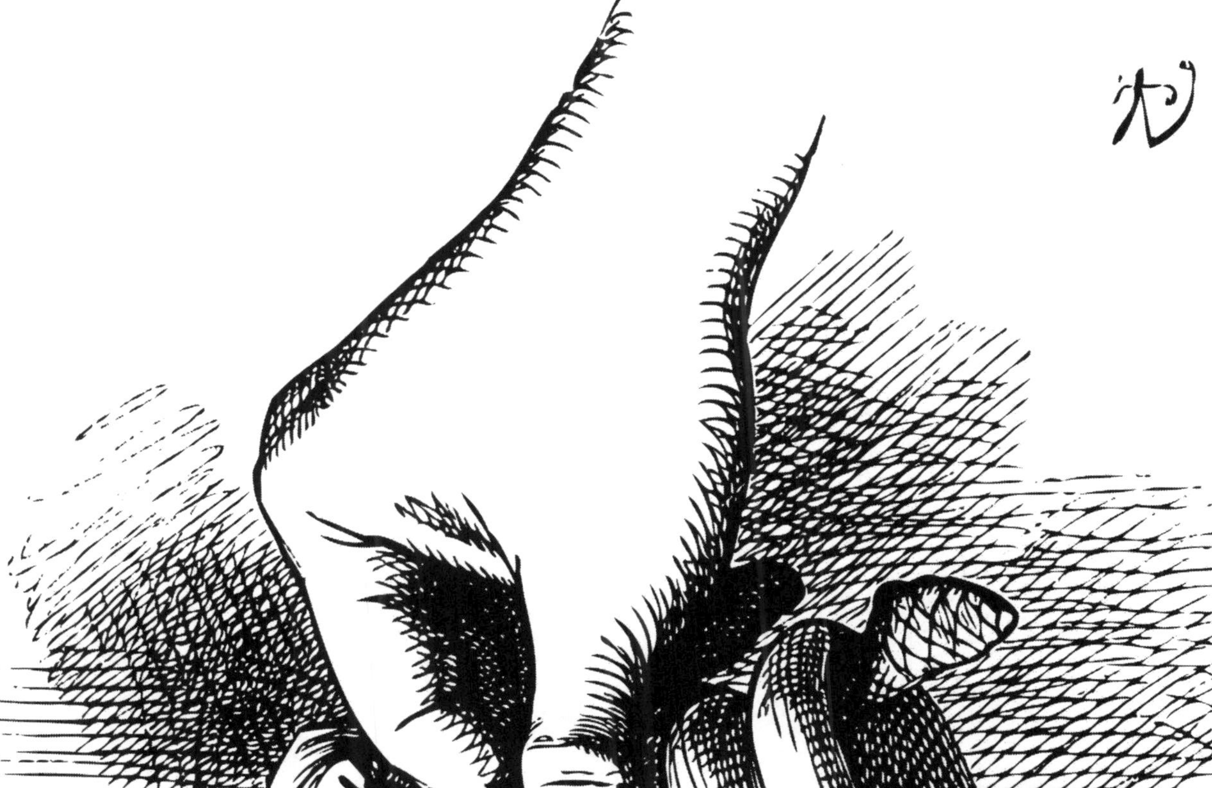

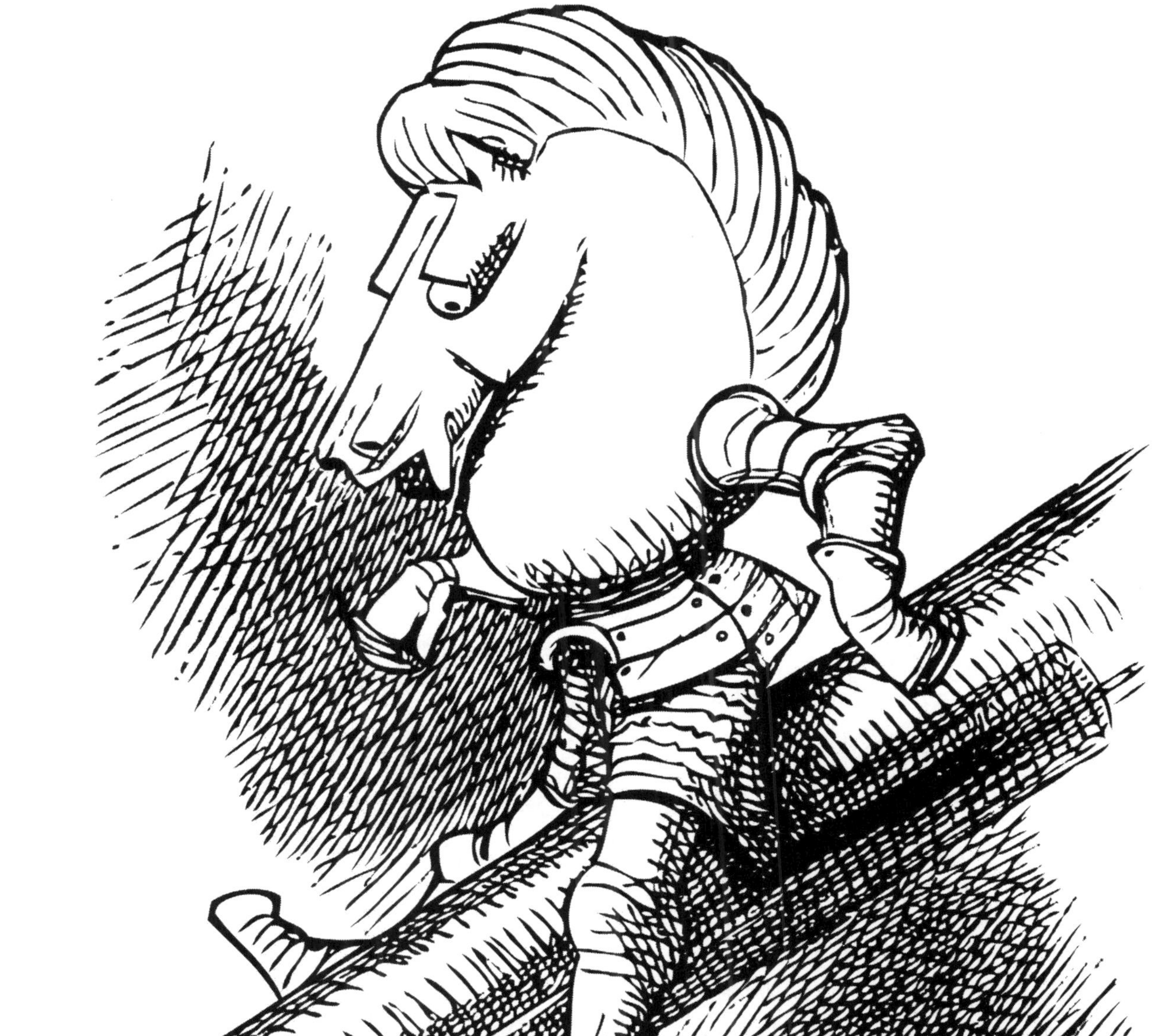

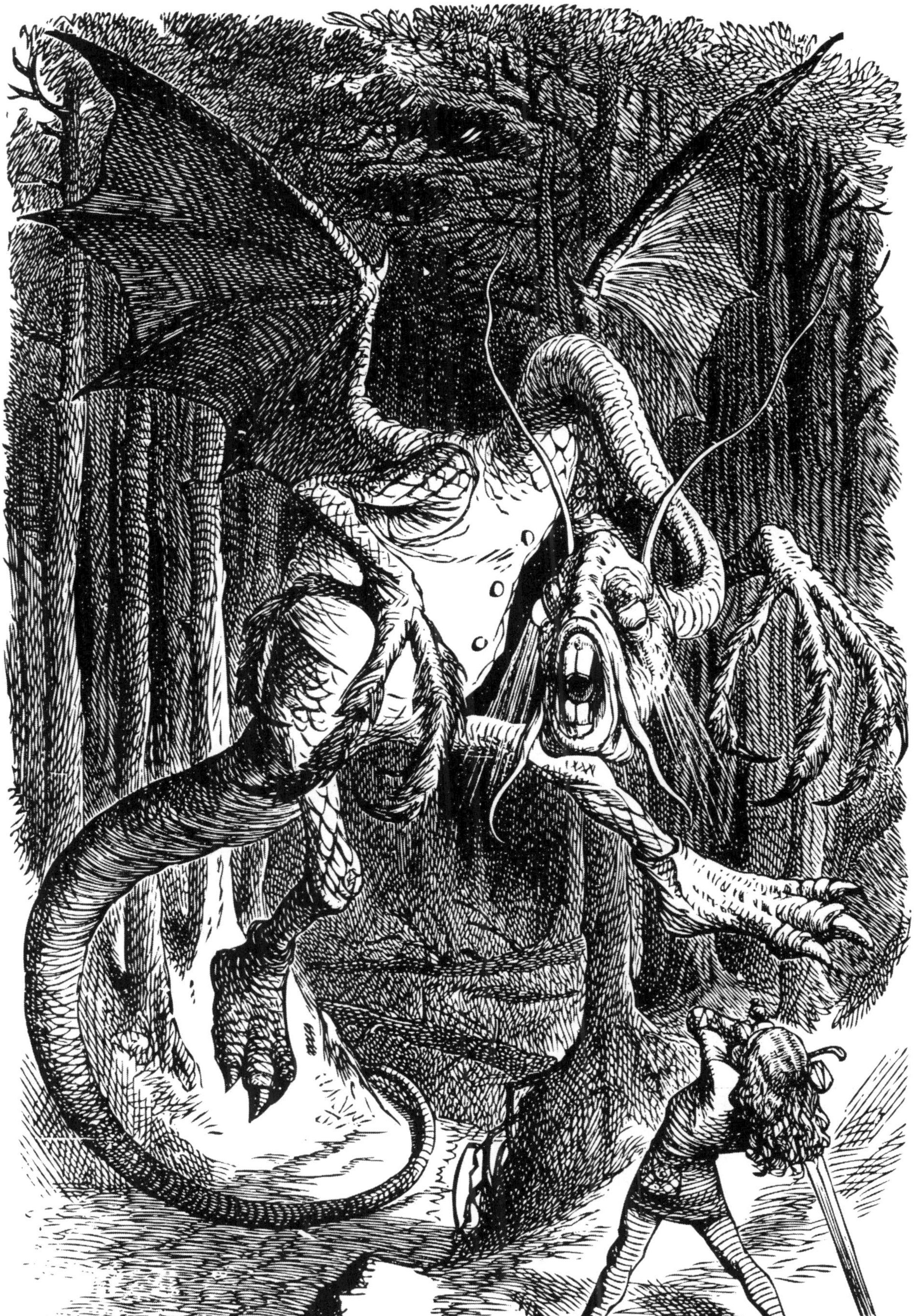

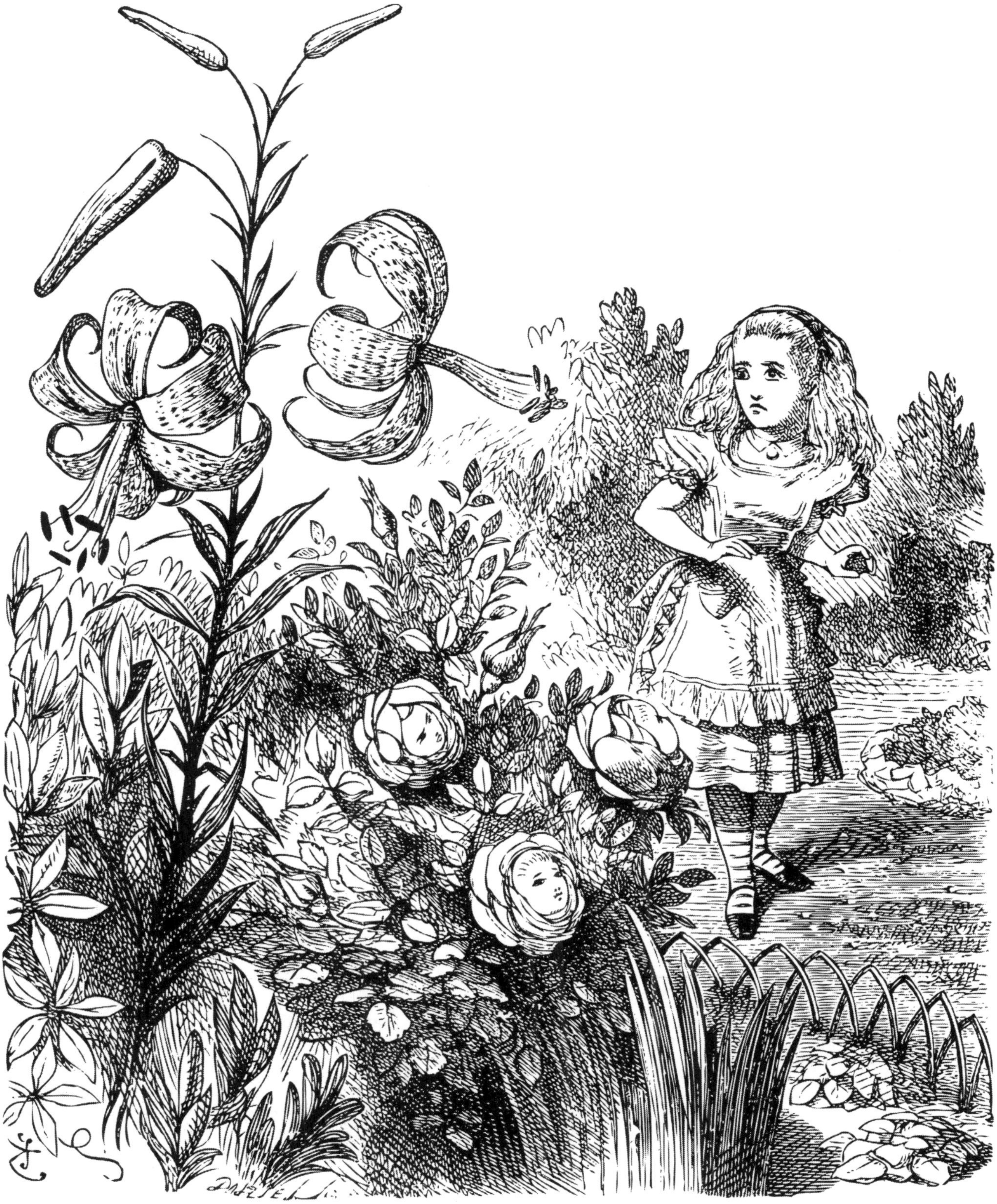

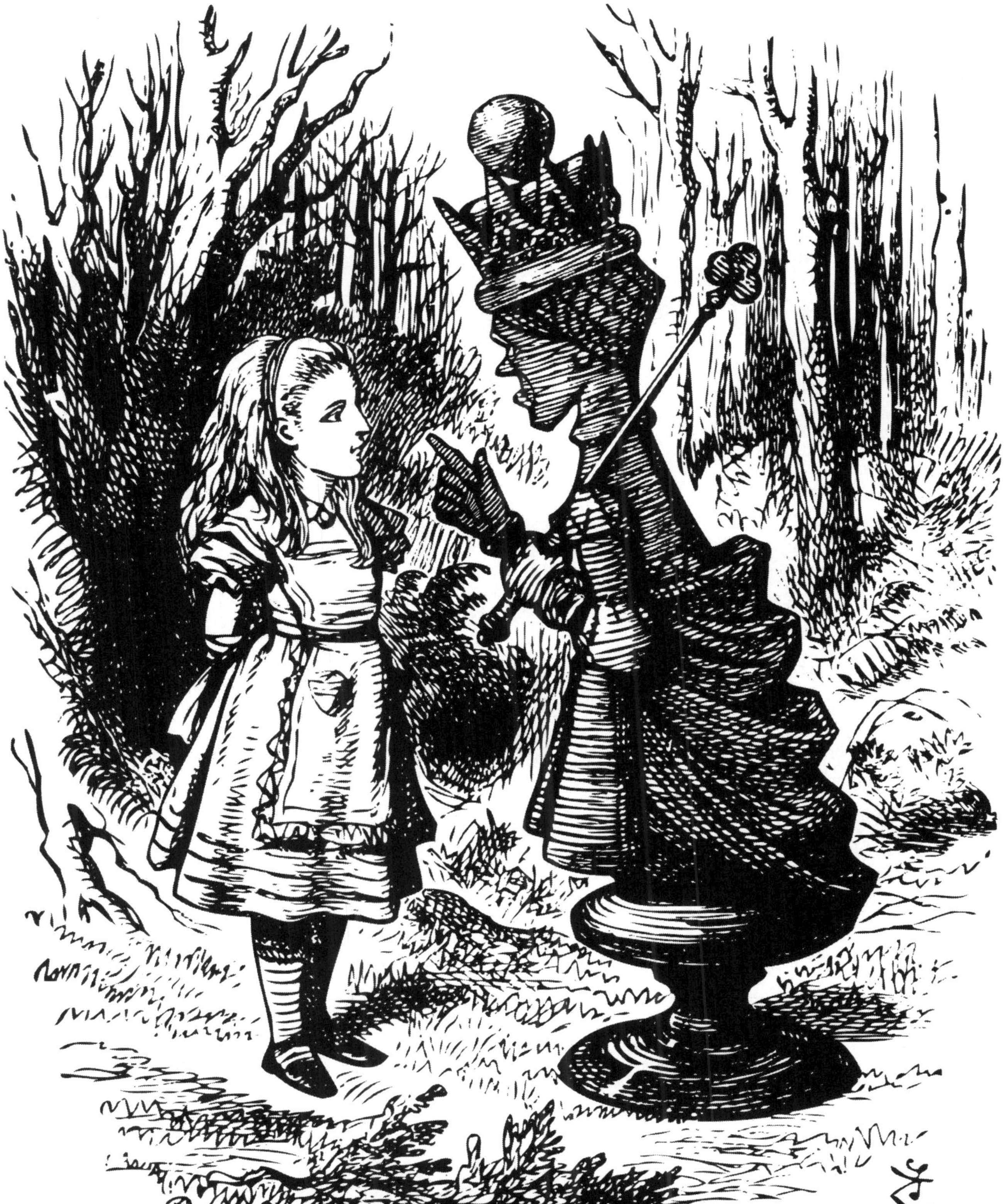

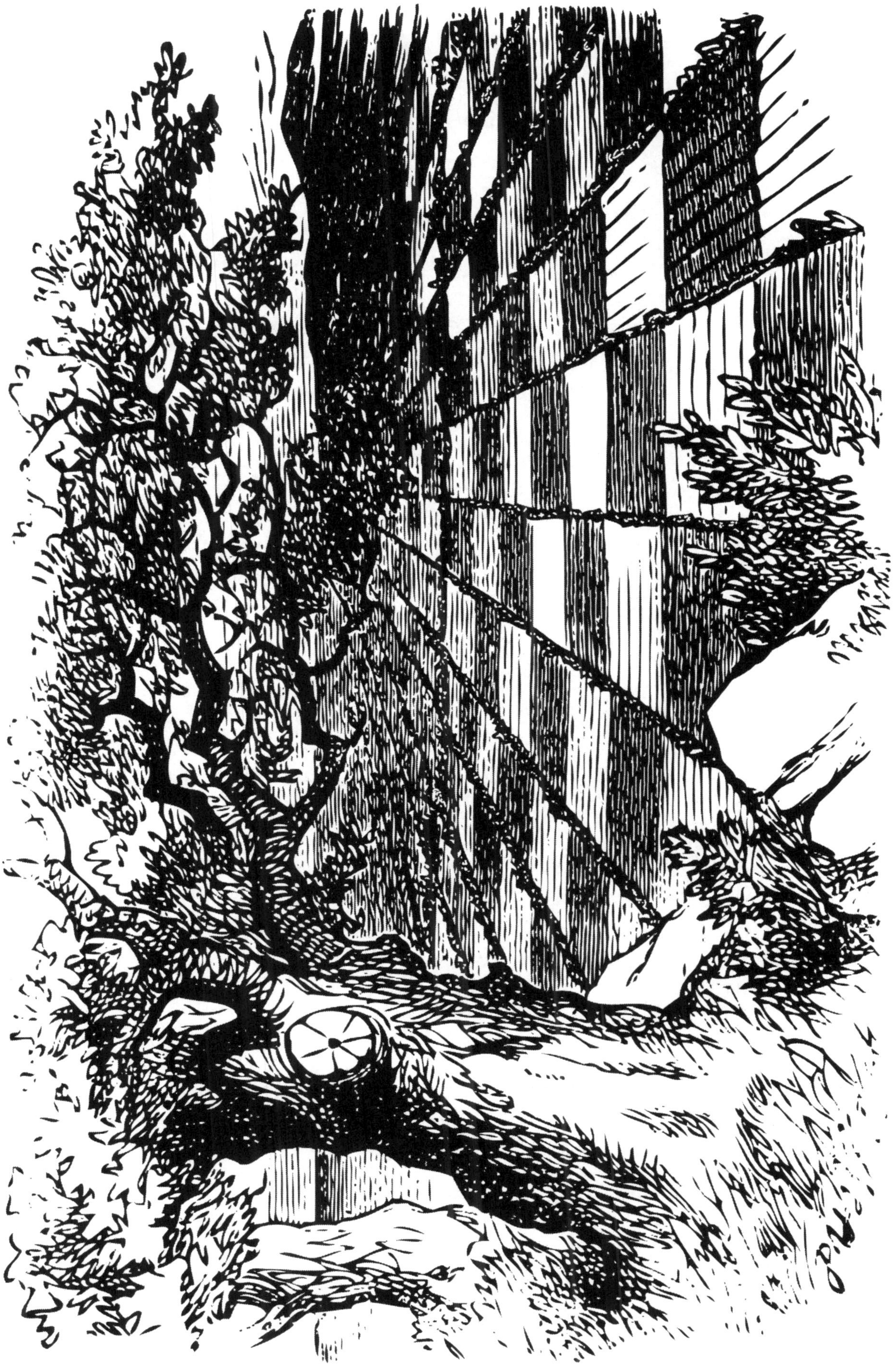

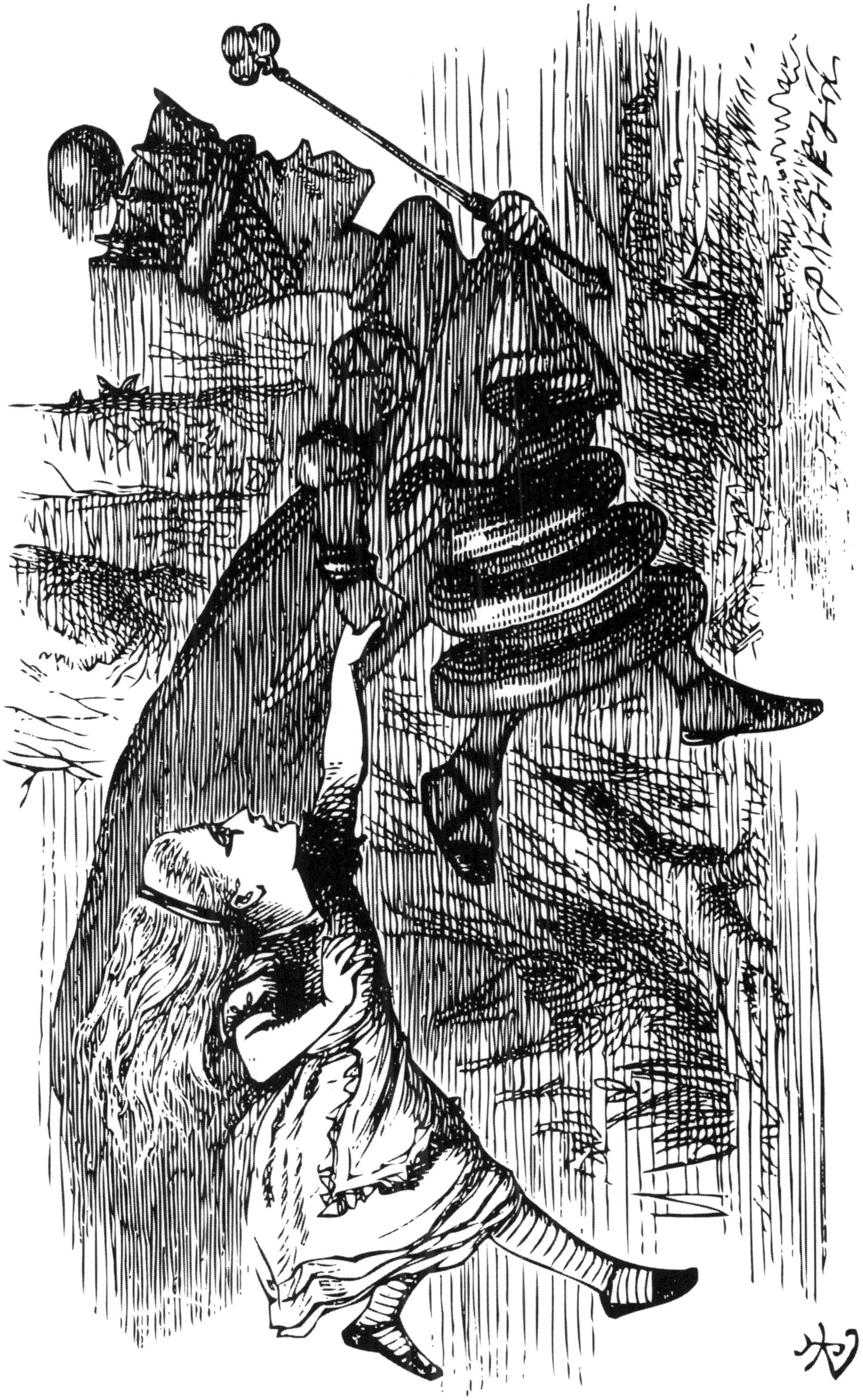

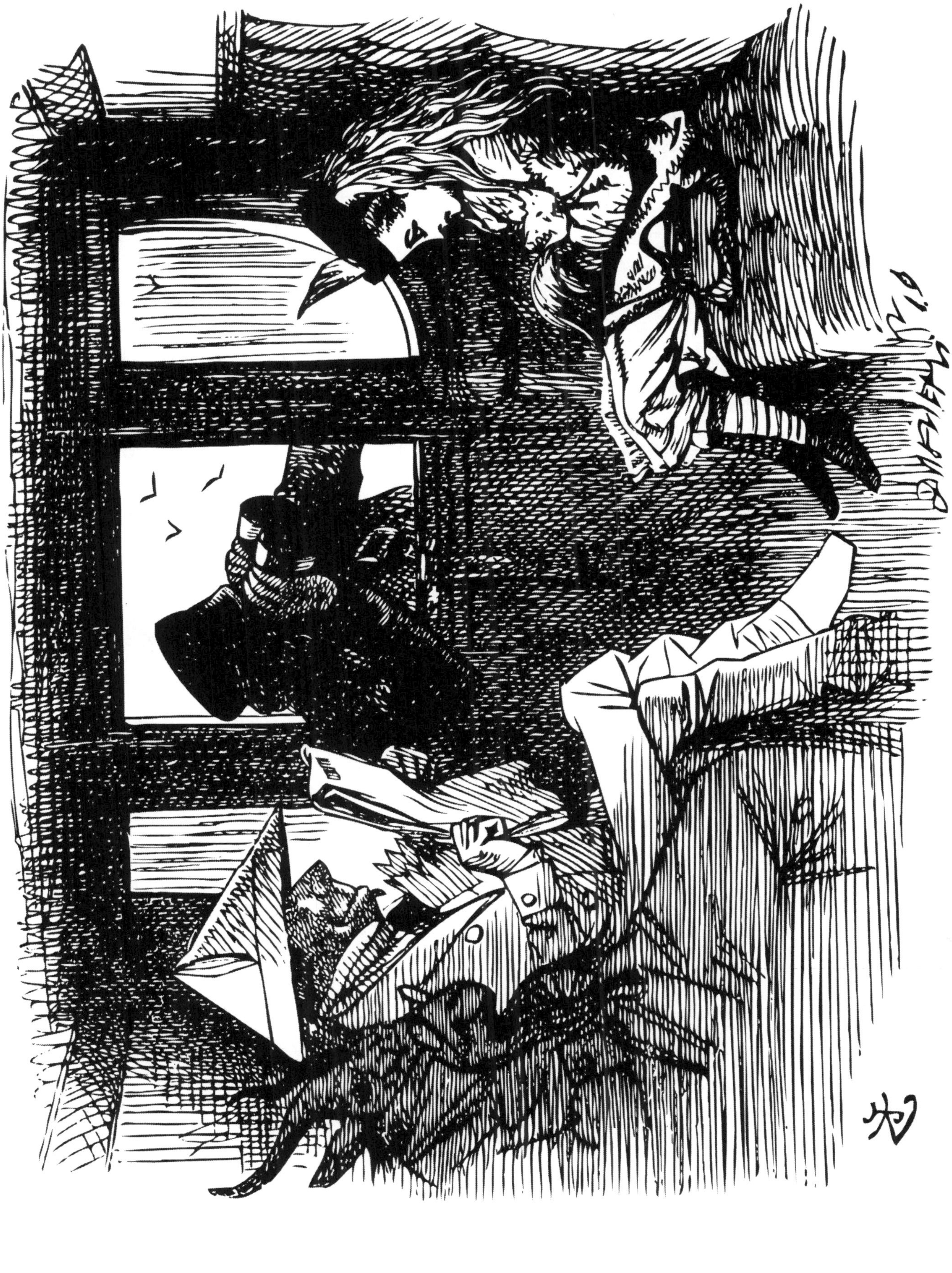

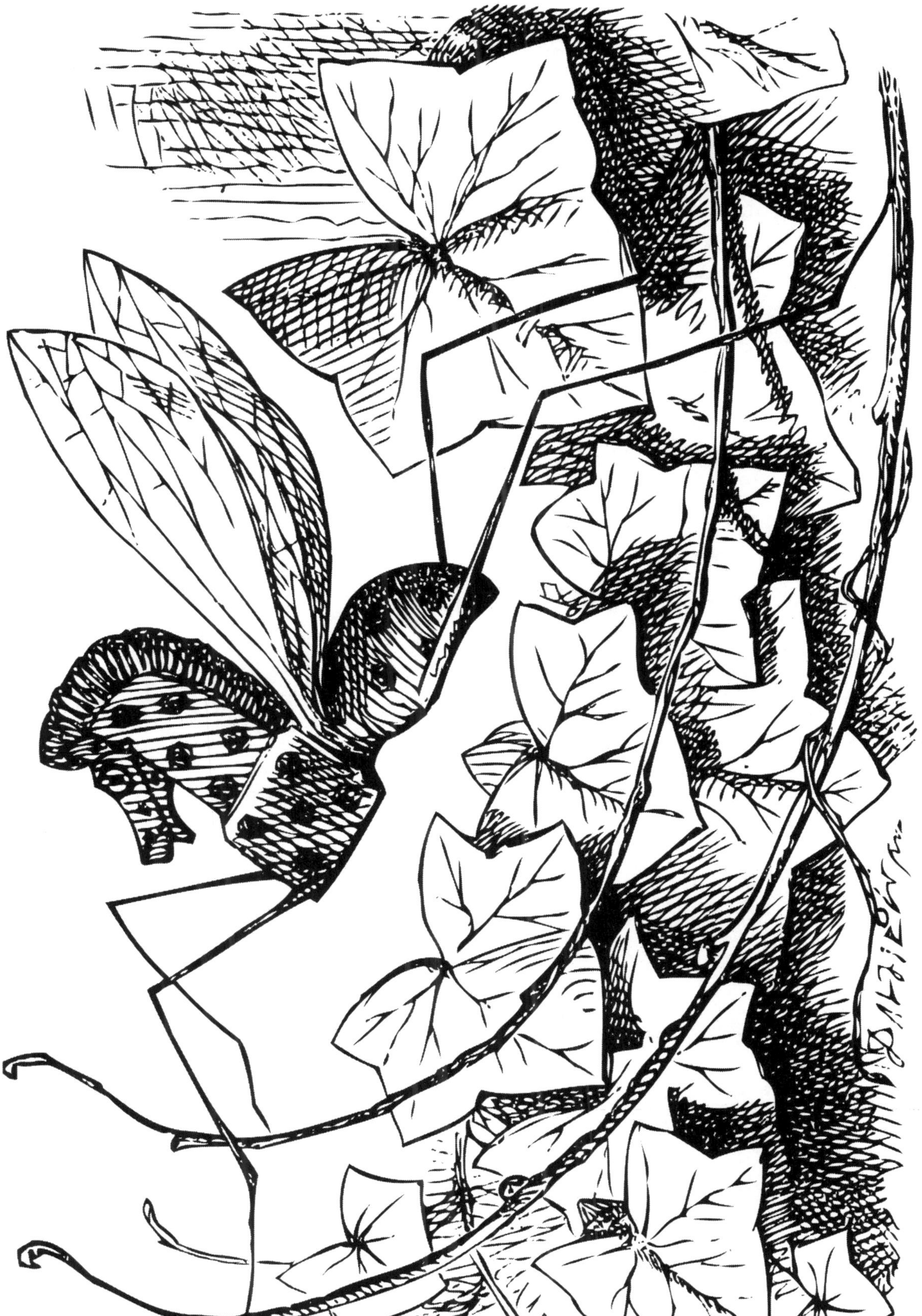

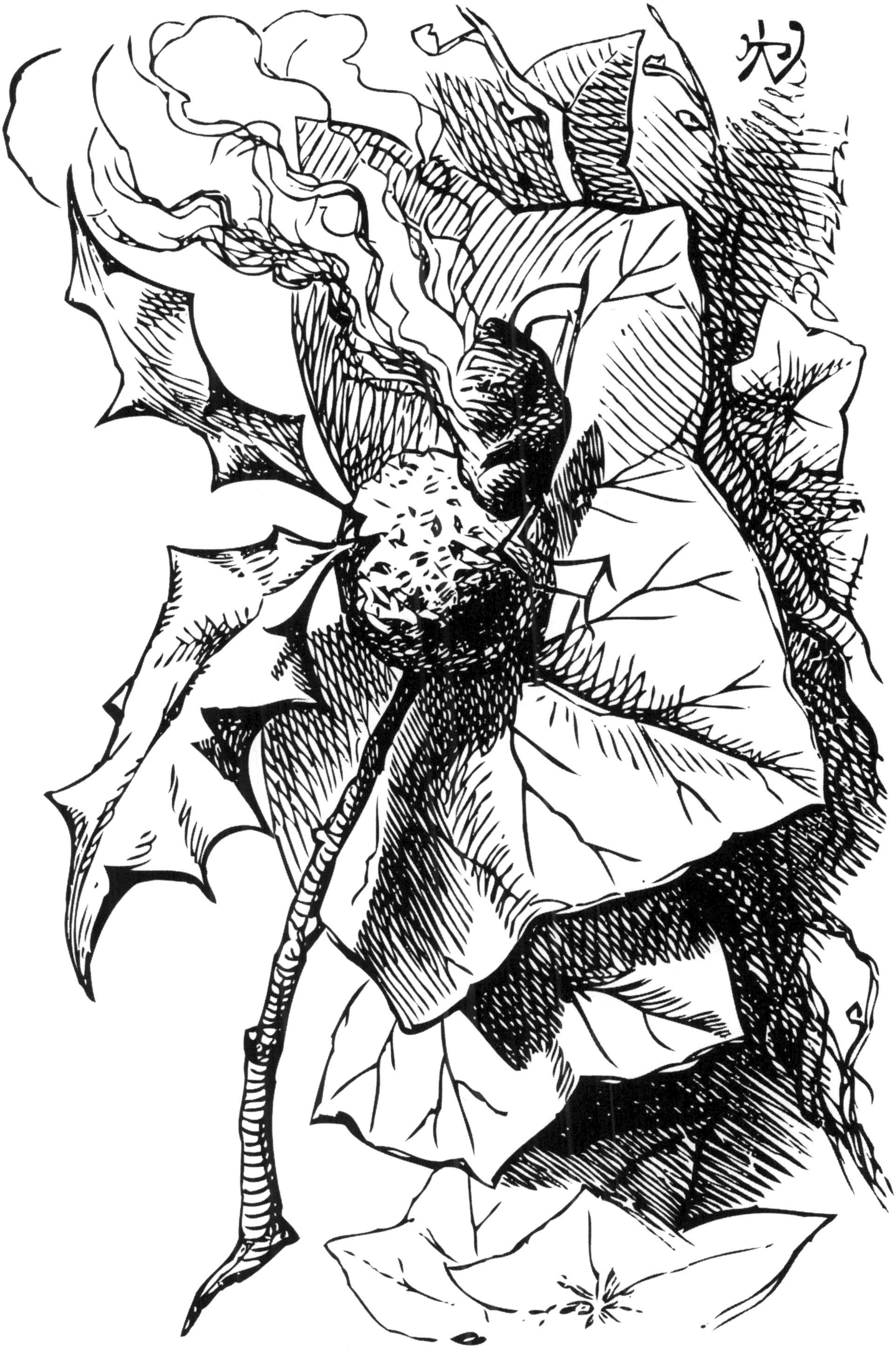

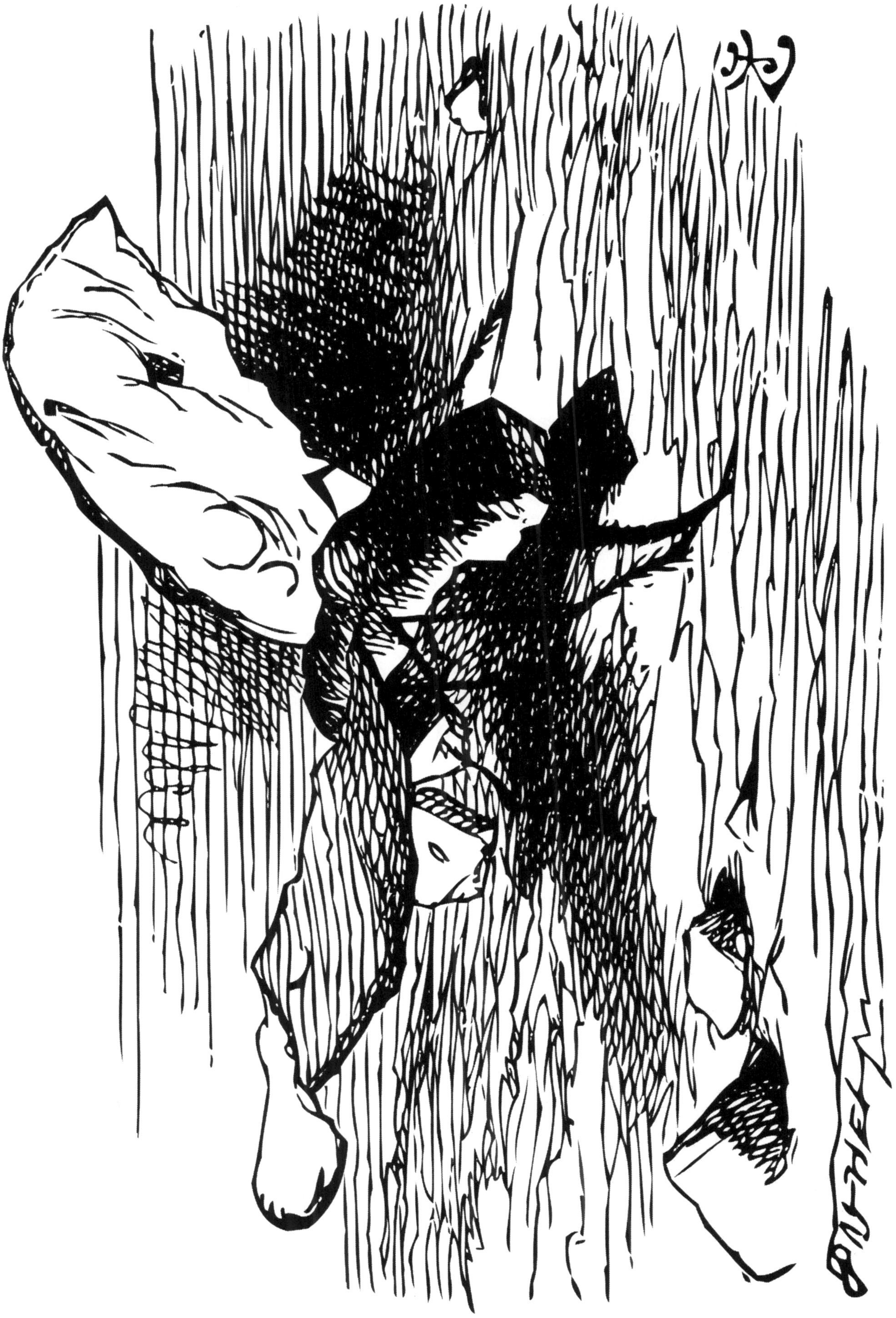

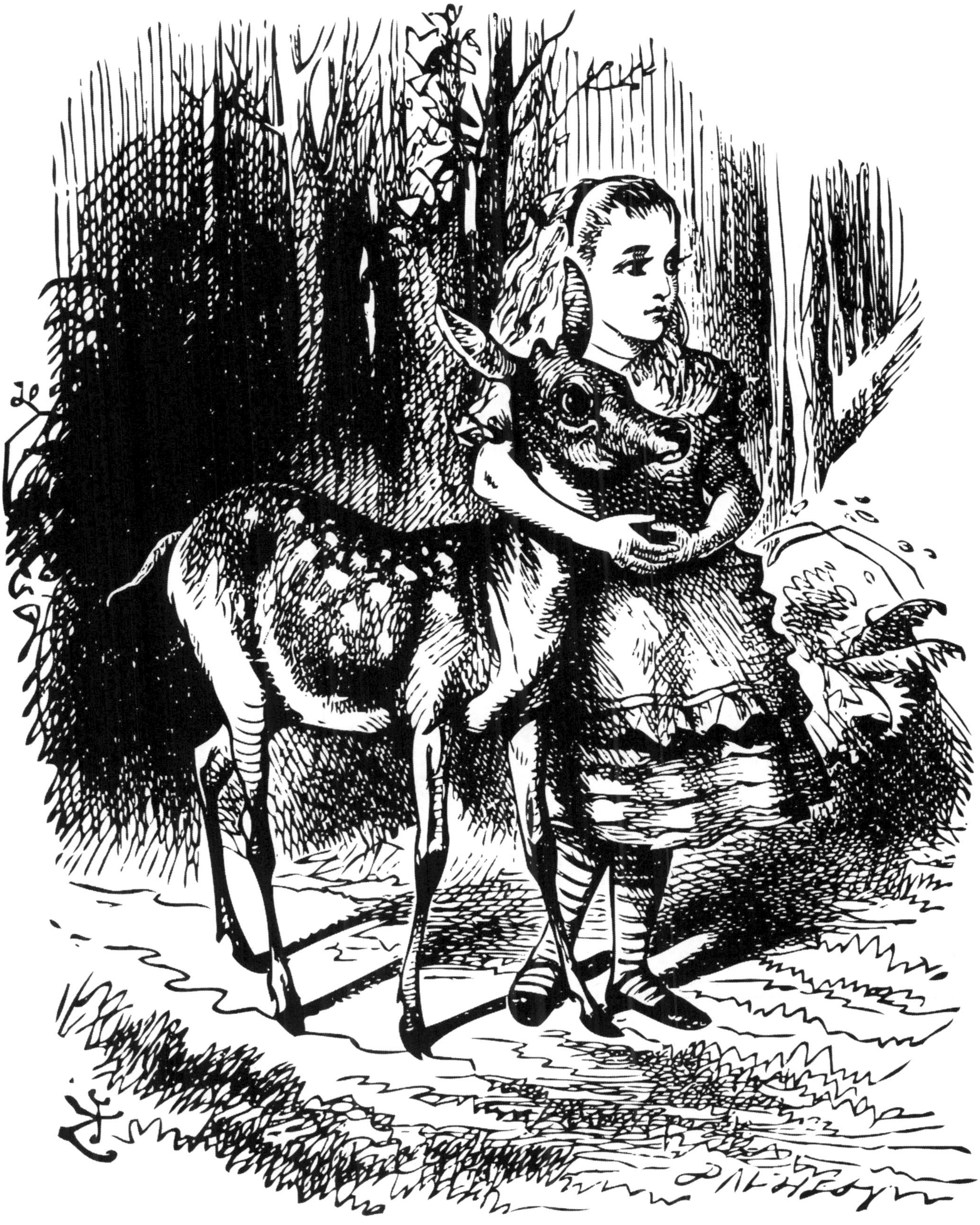

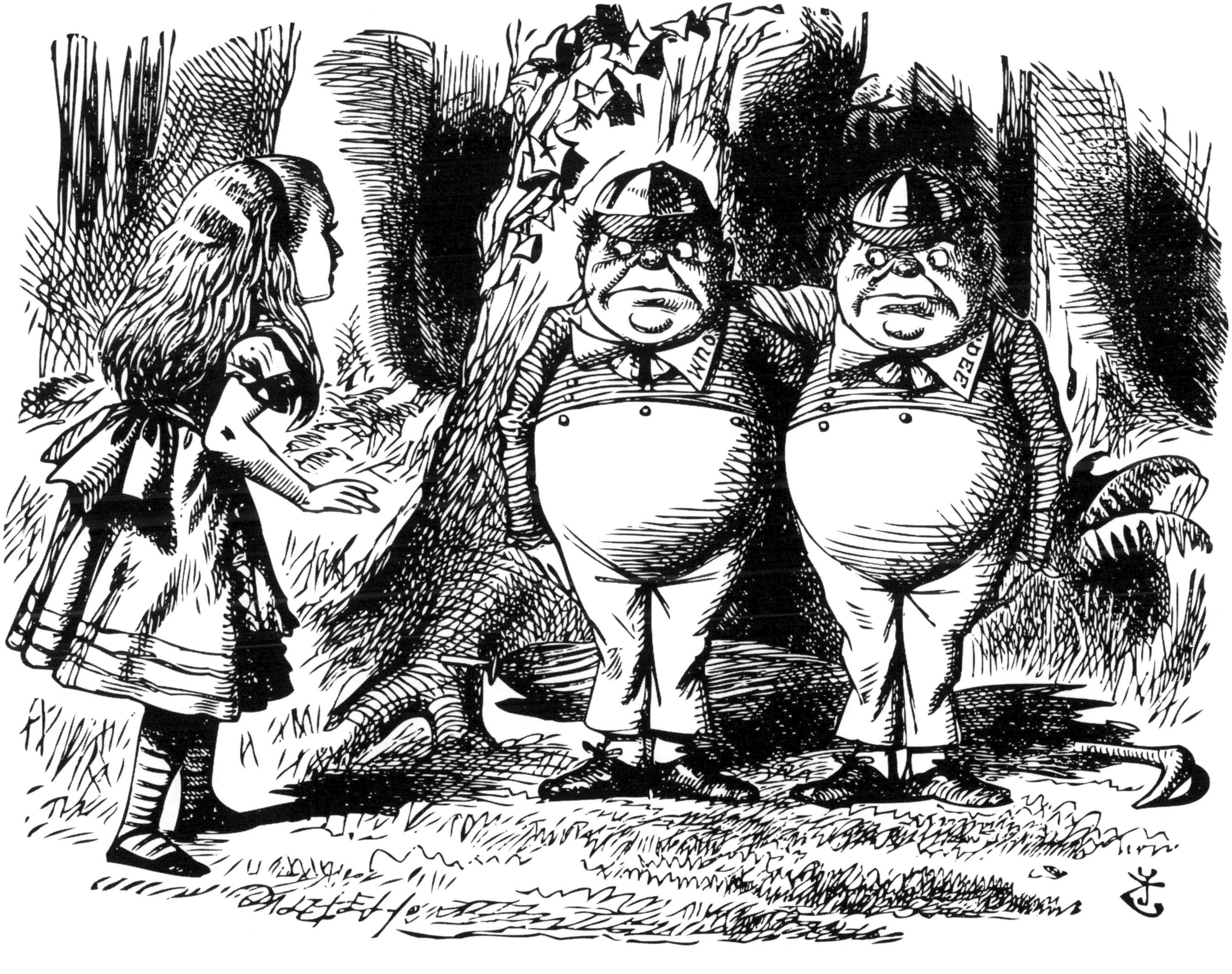
DUM
DEE

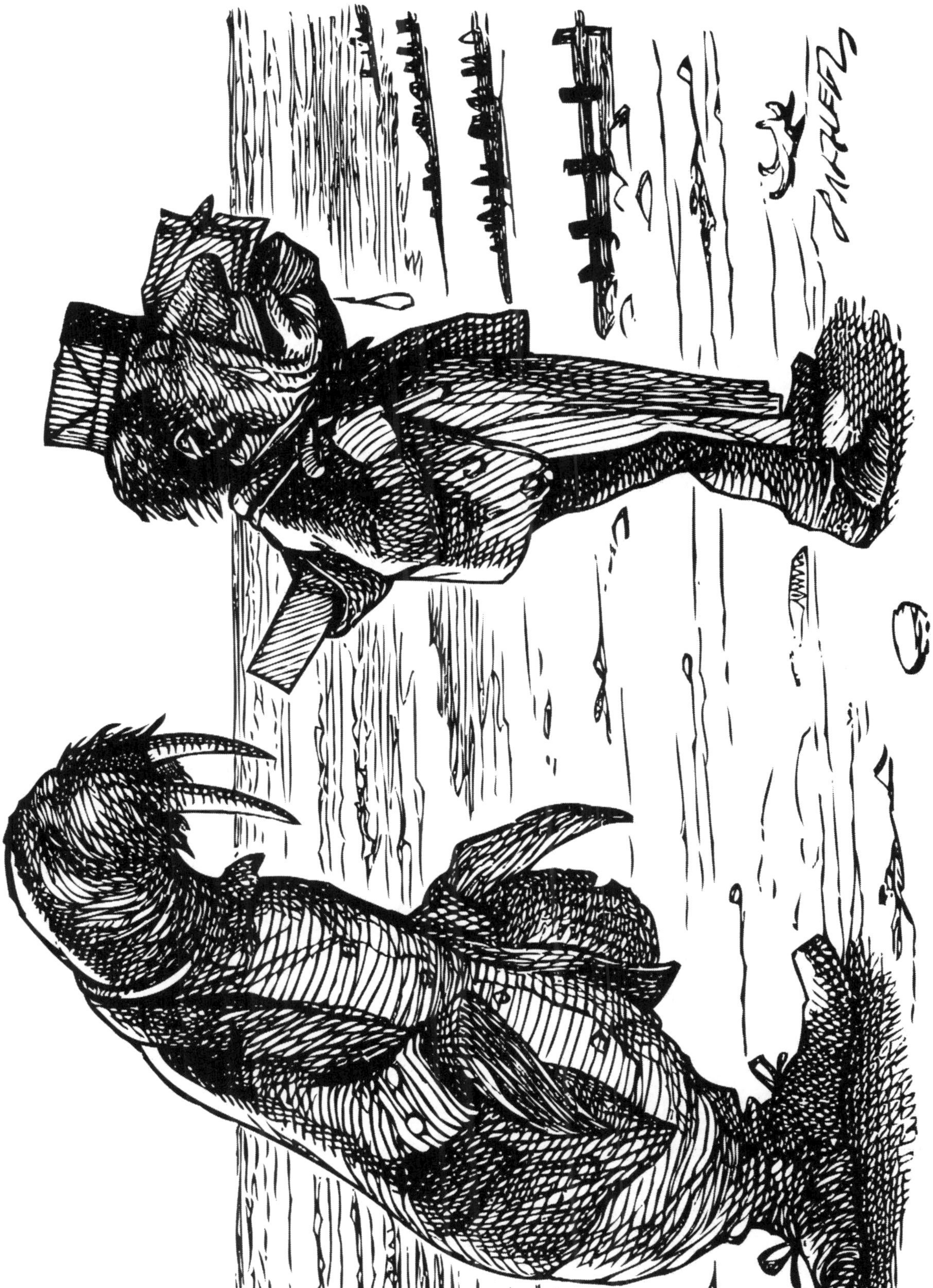

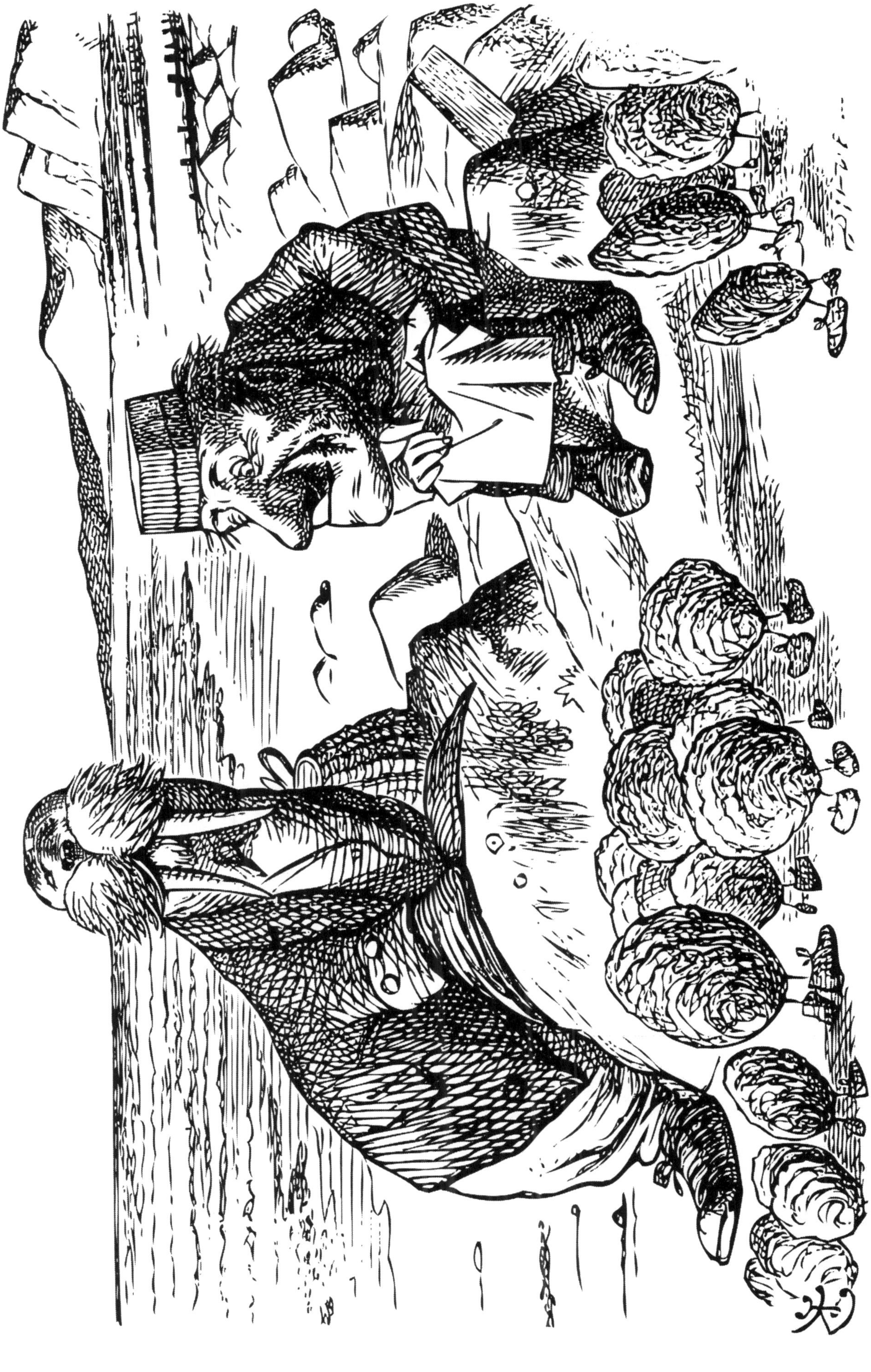

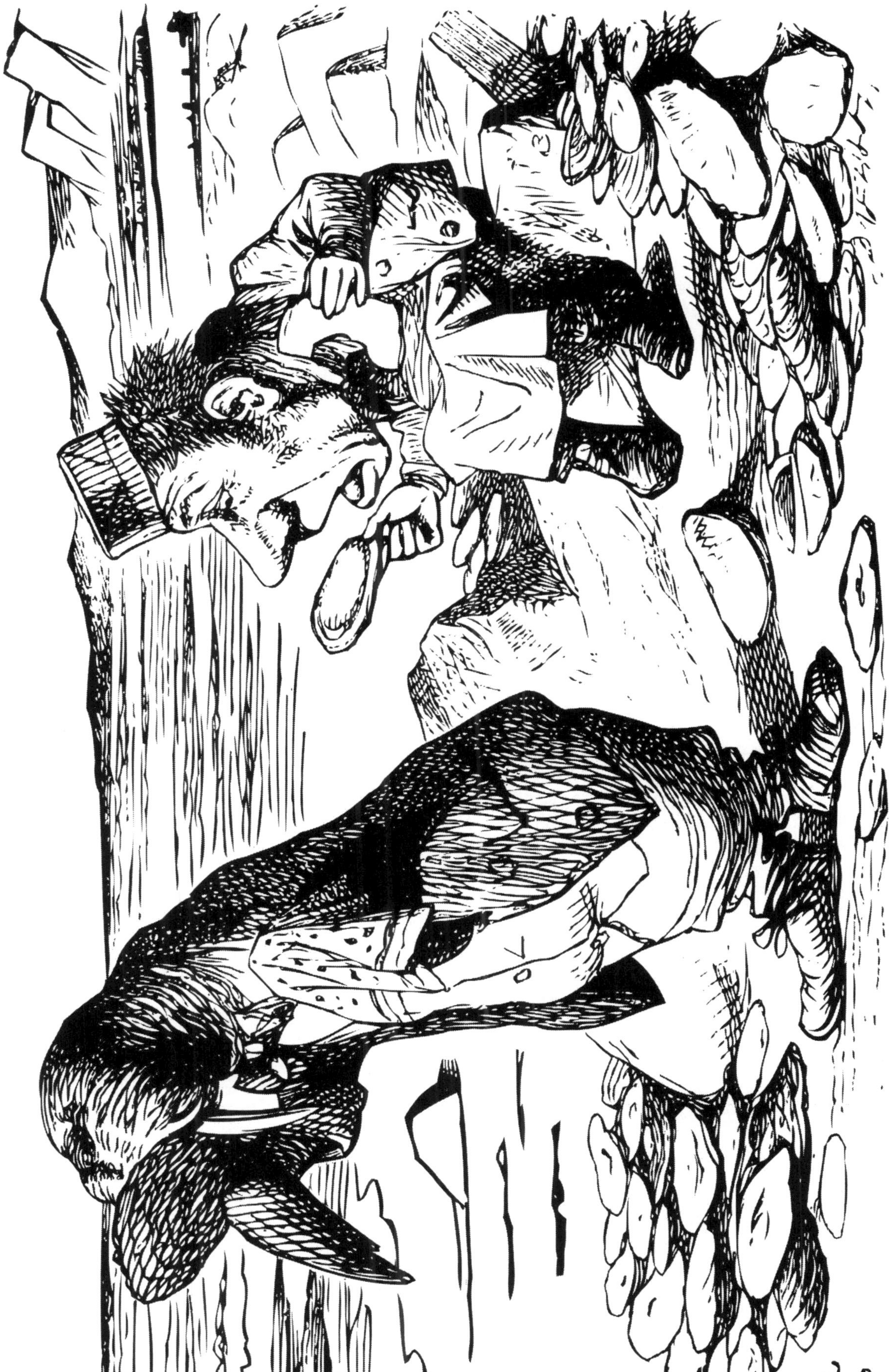

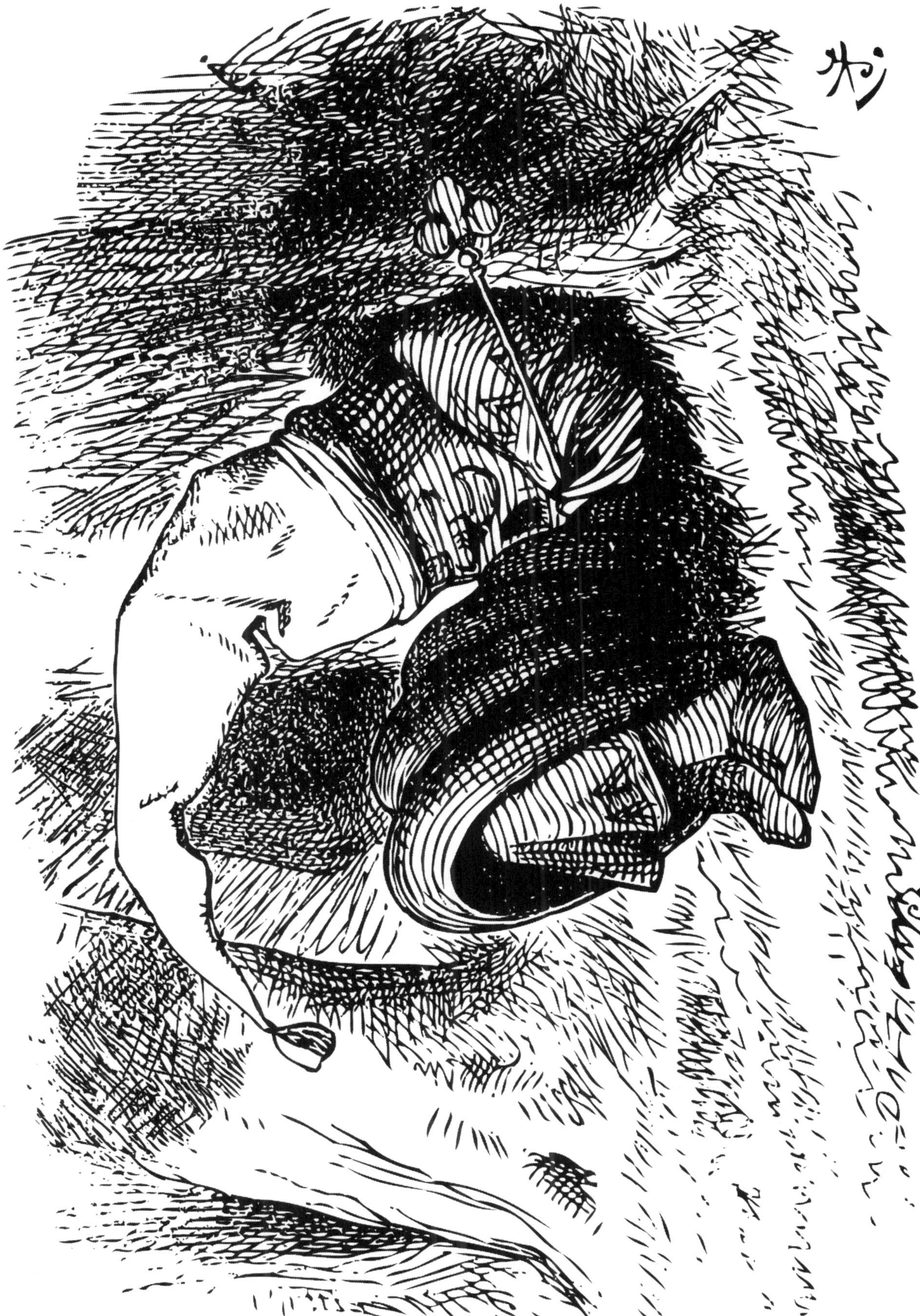

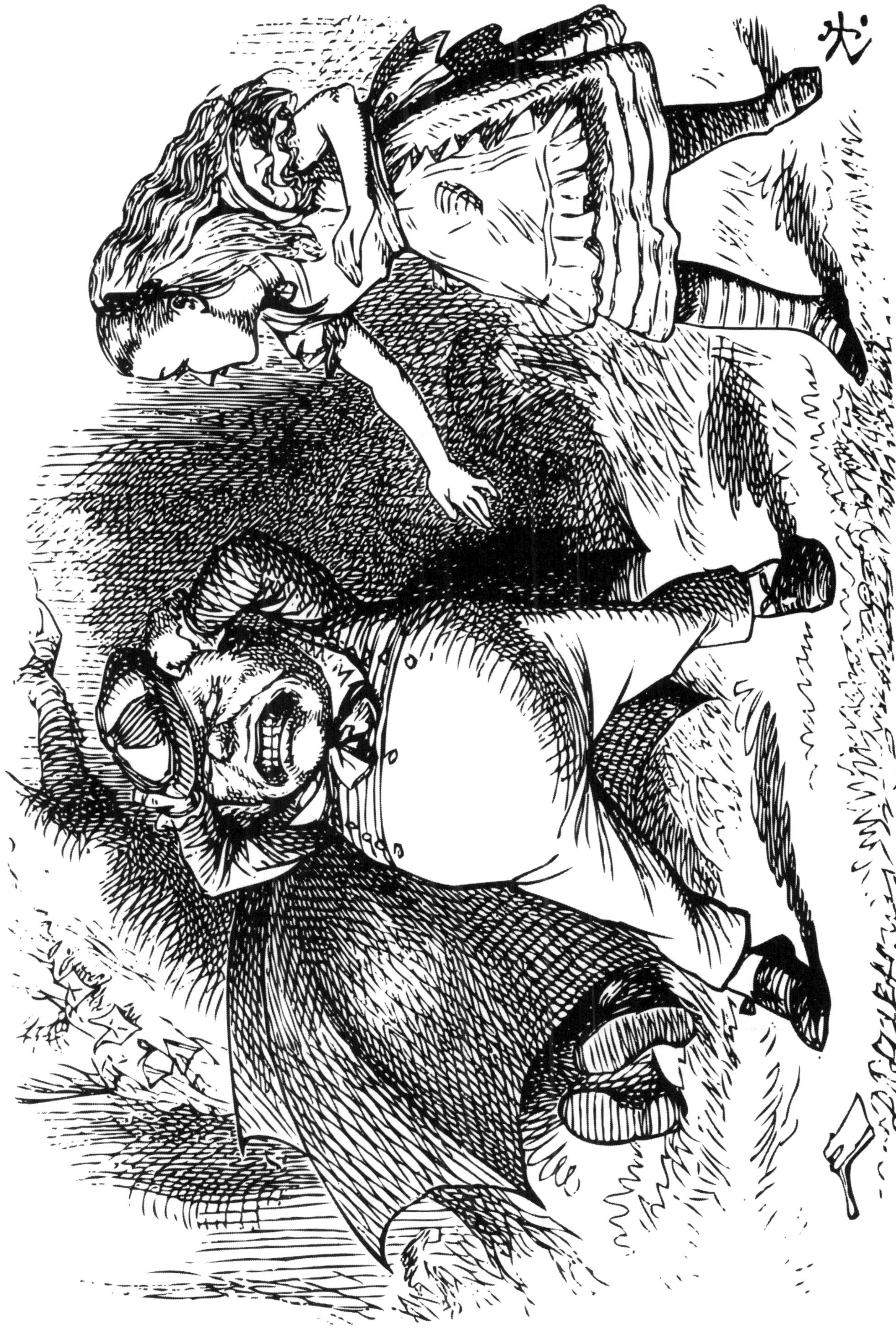

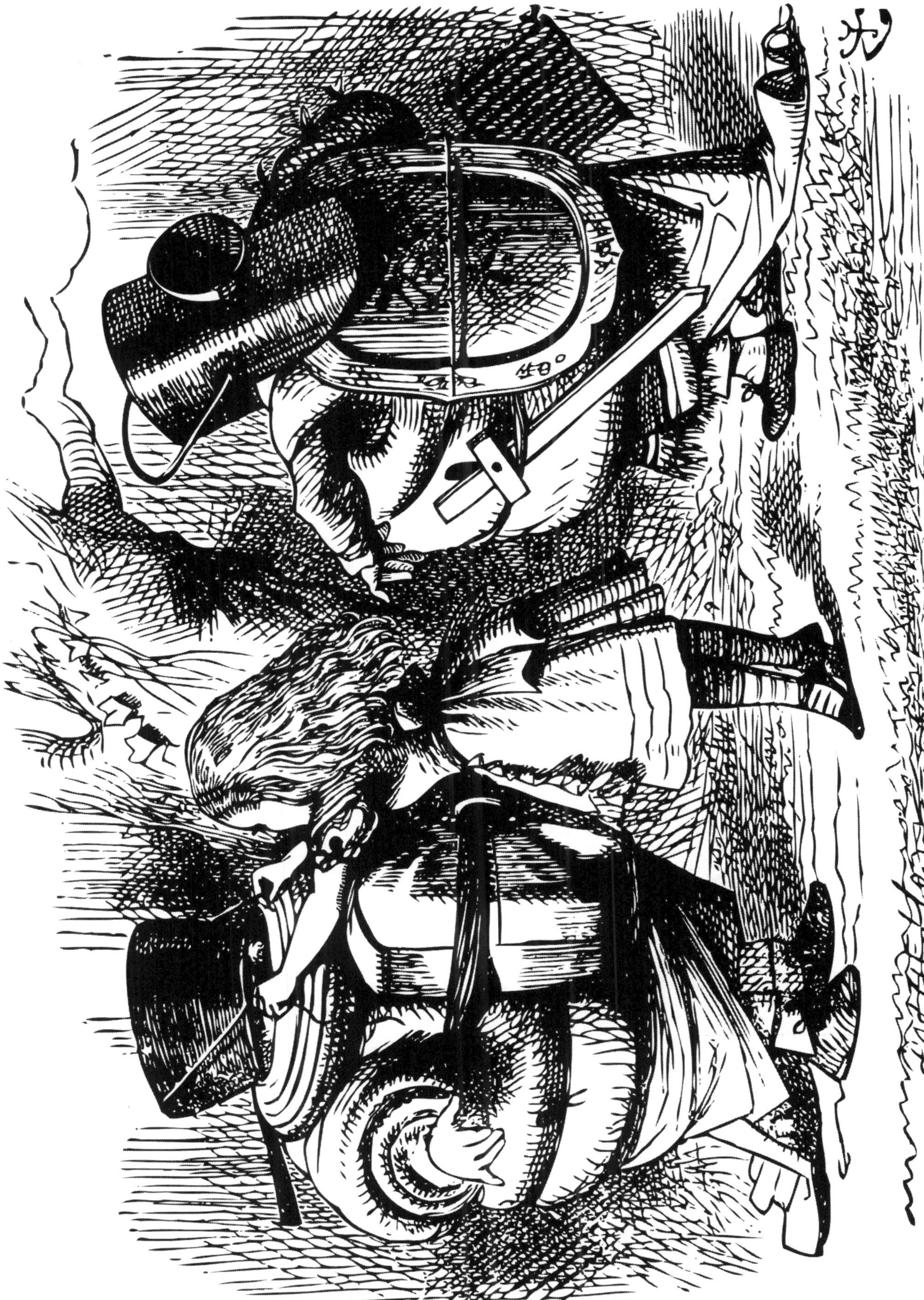

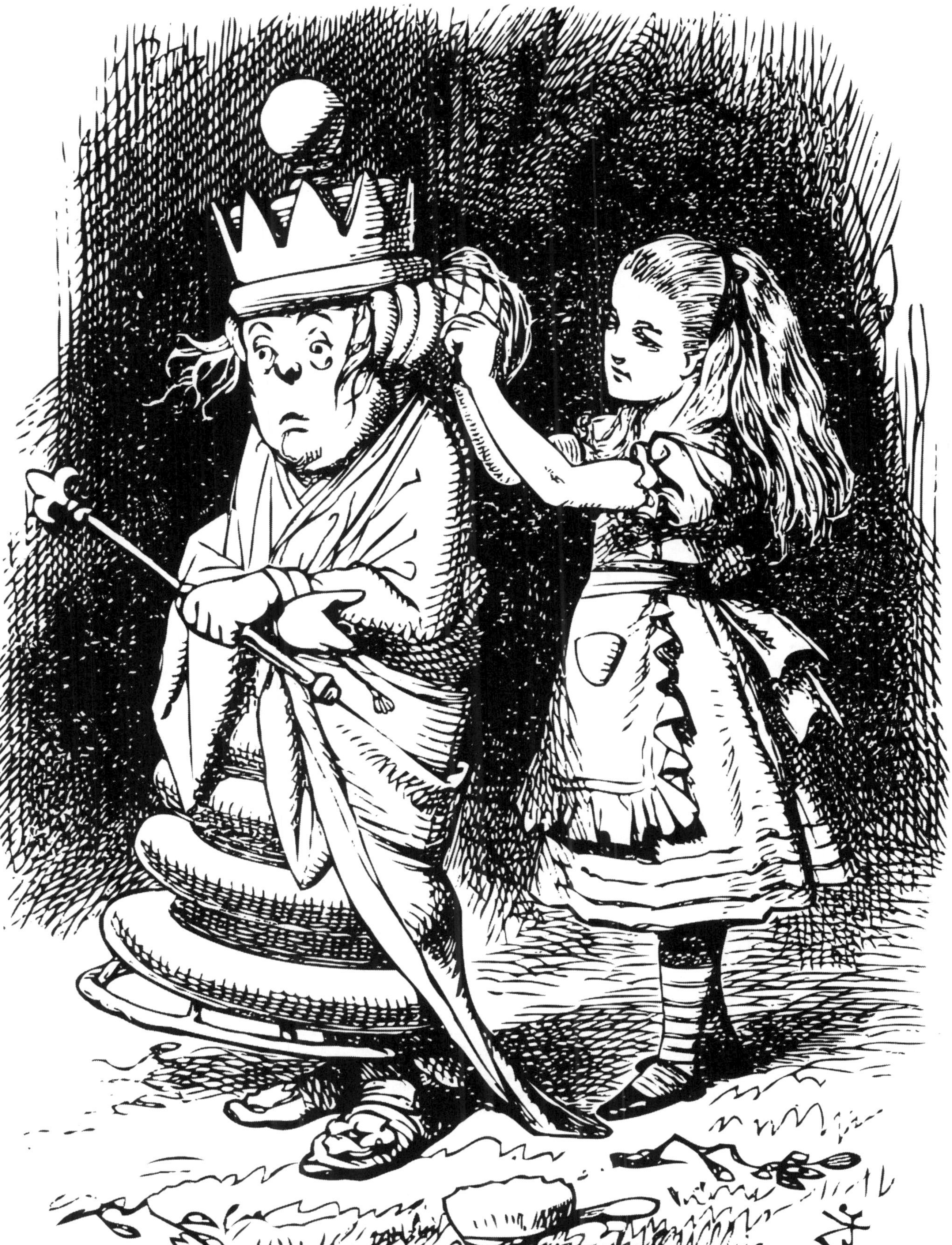

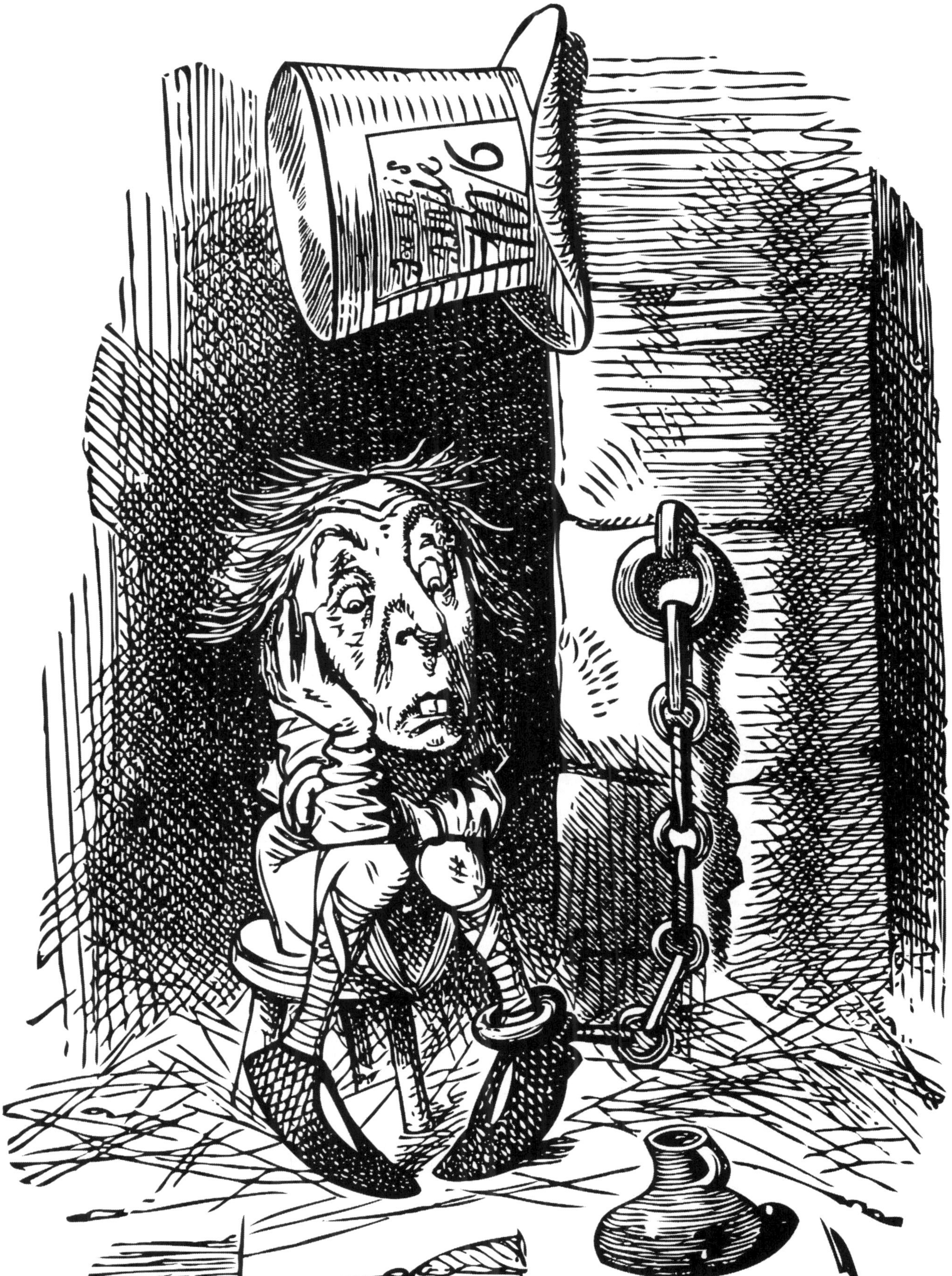

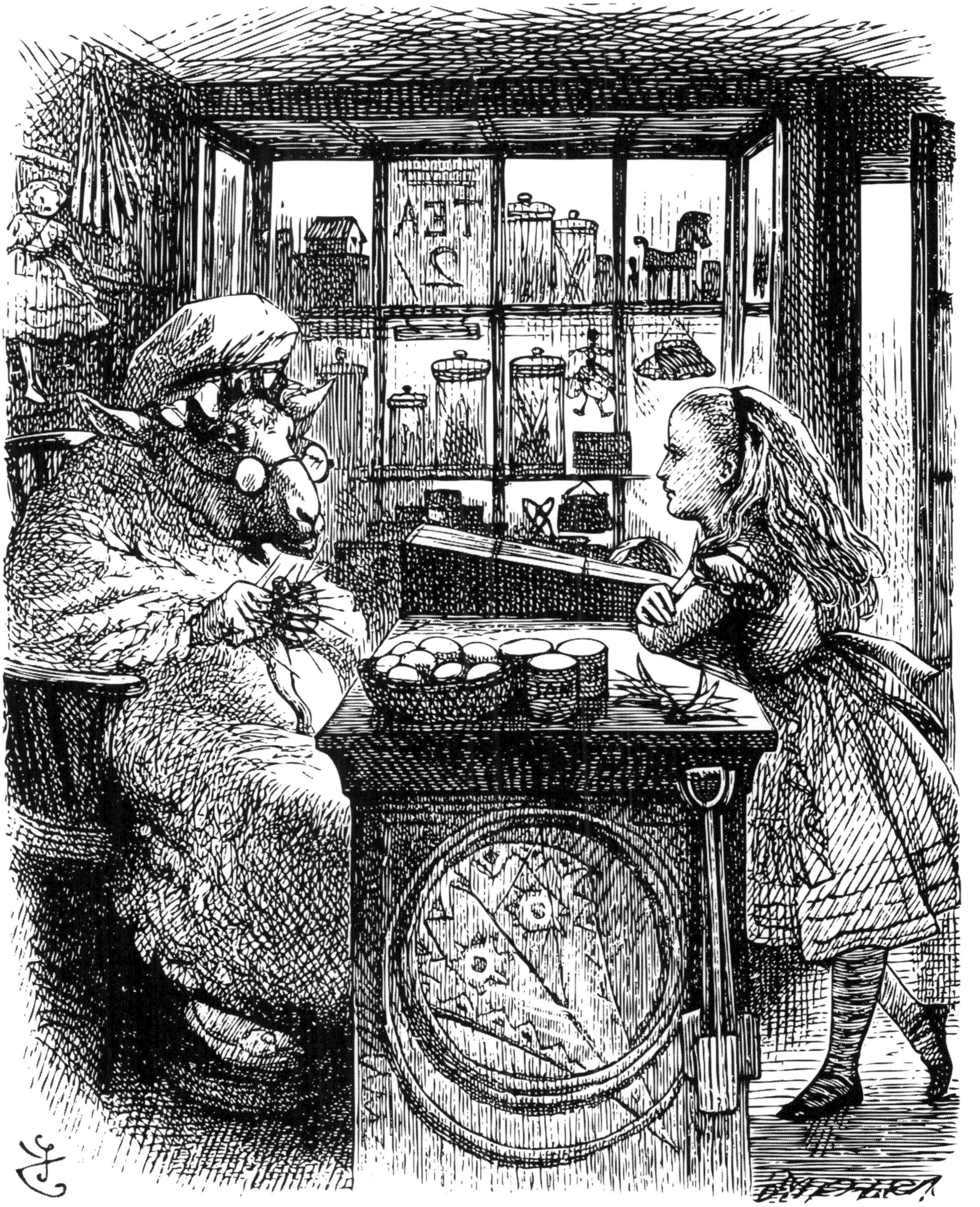

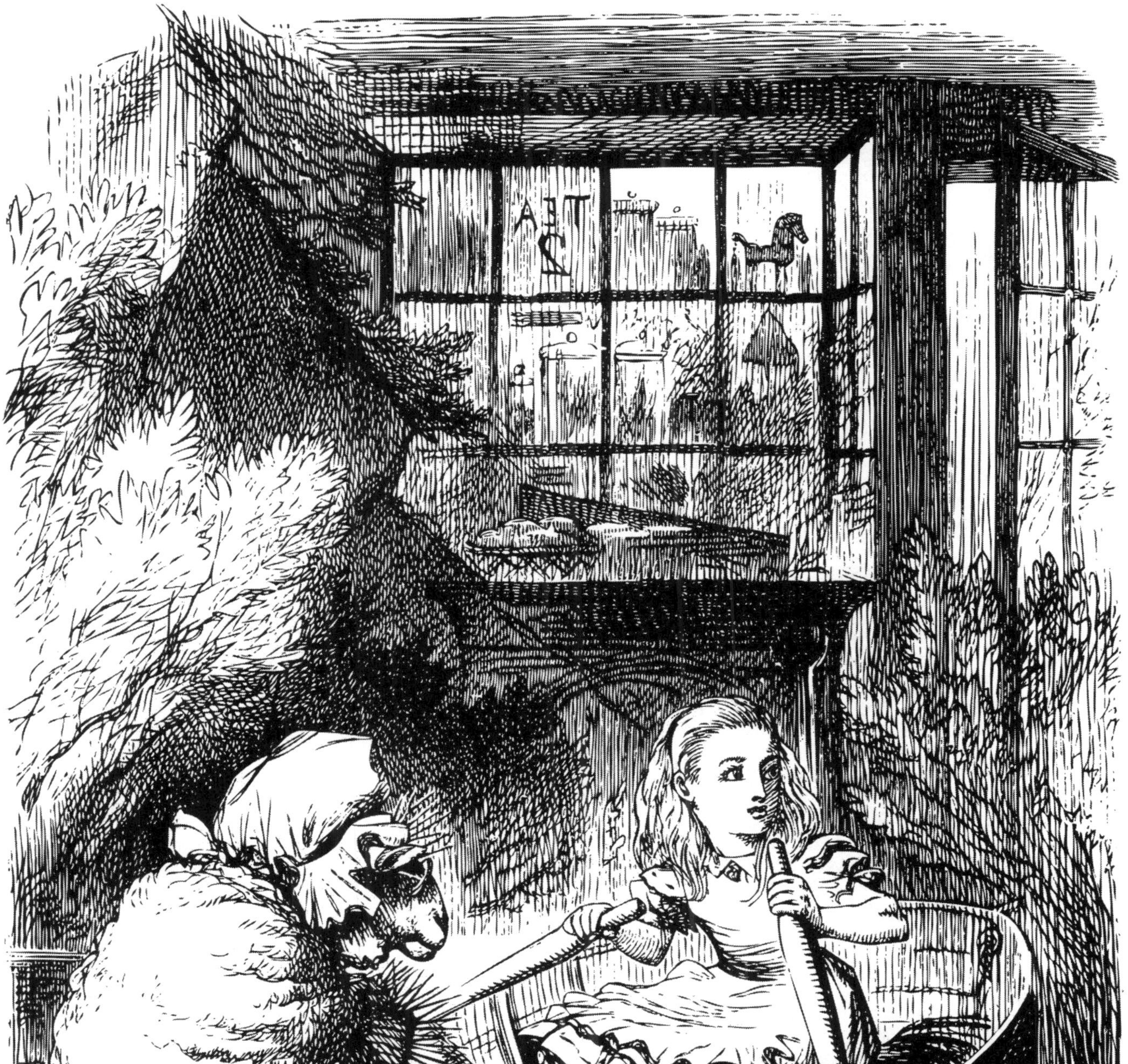
TEA

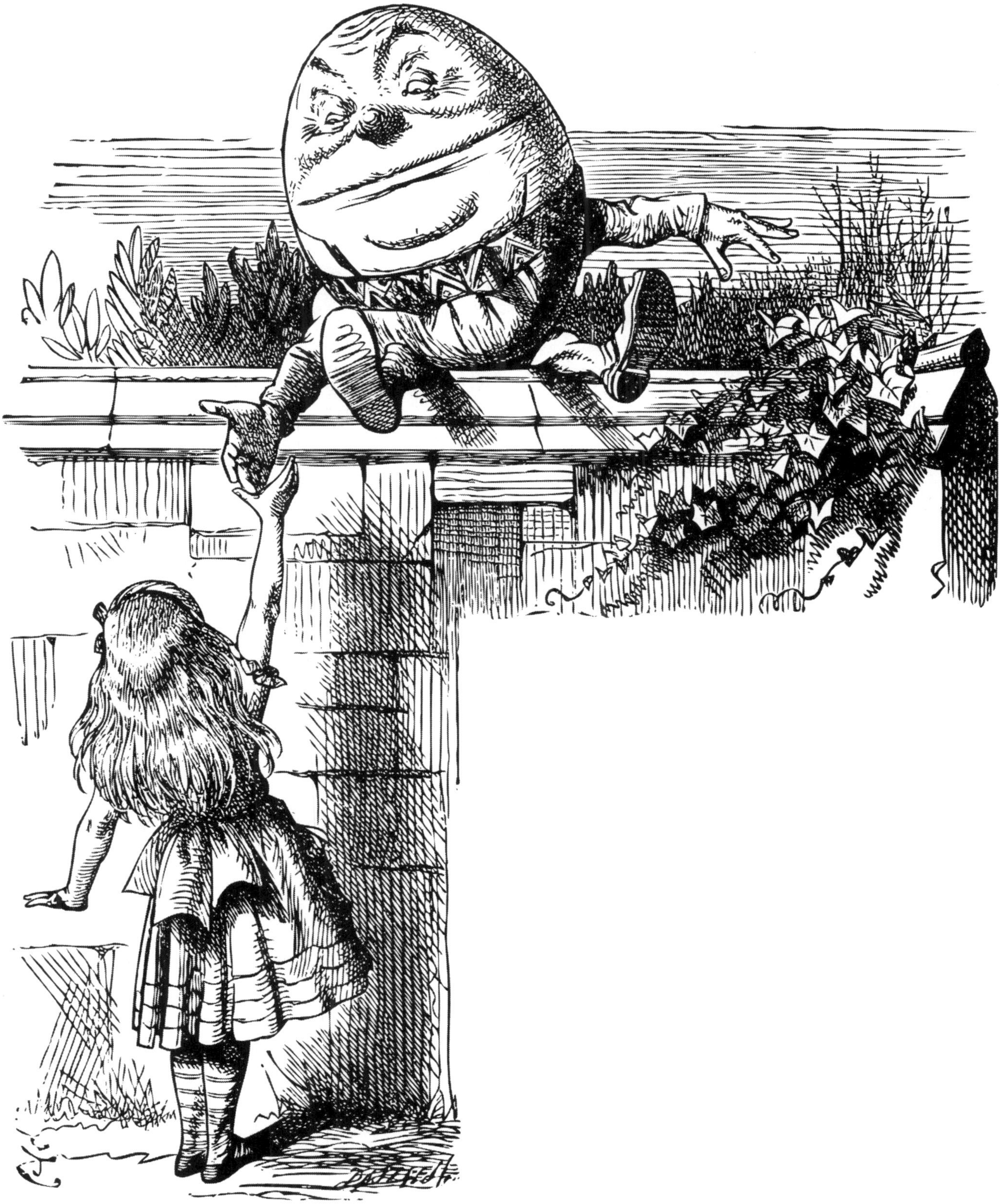

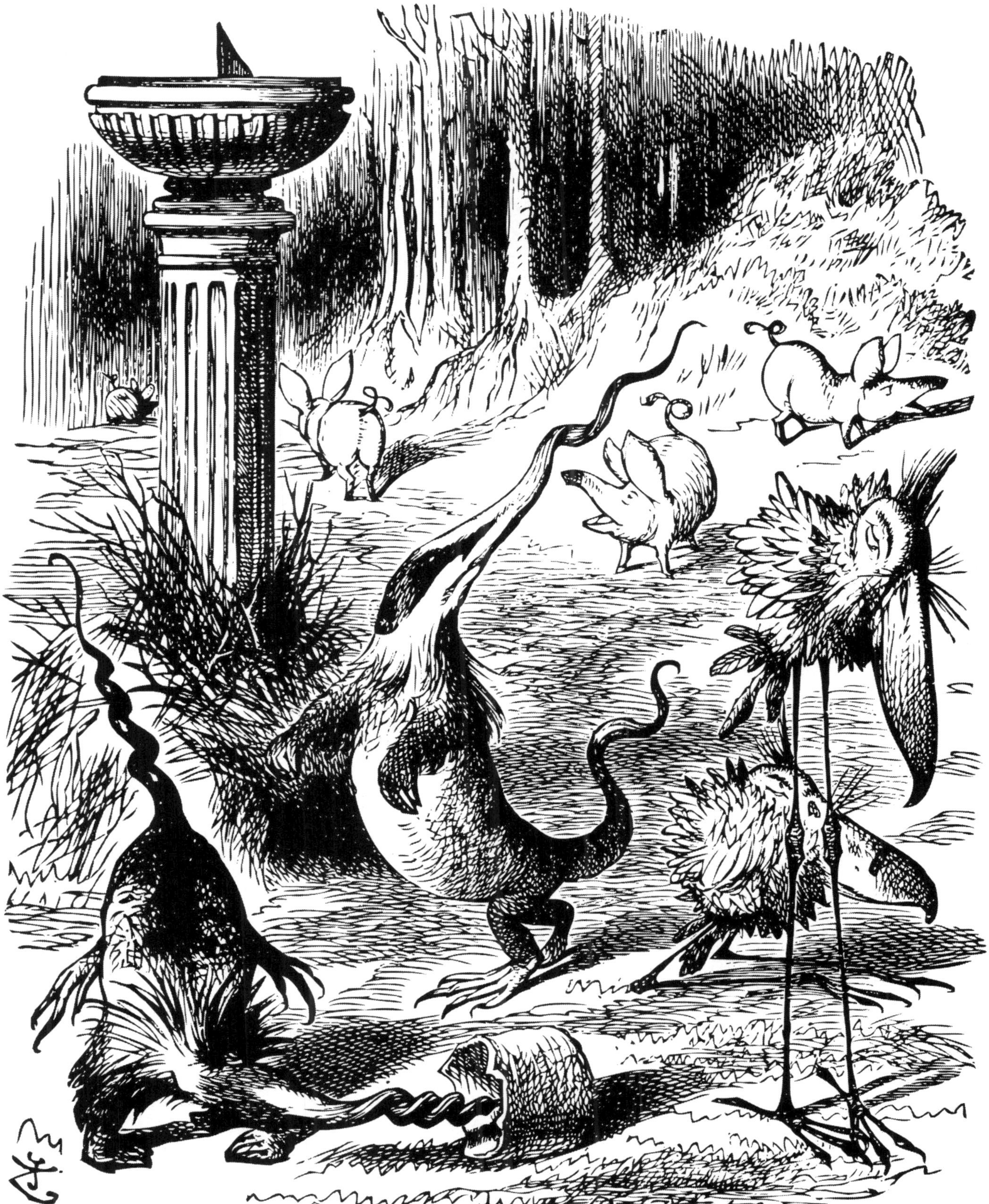

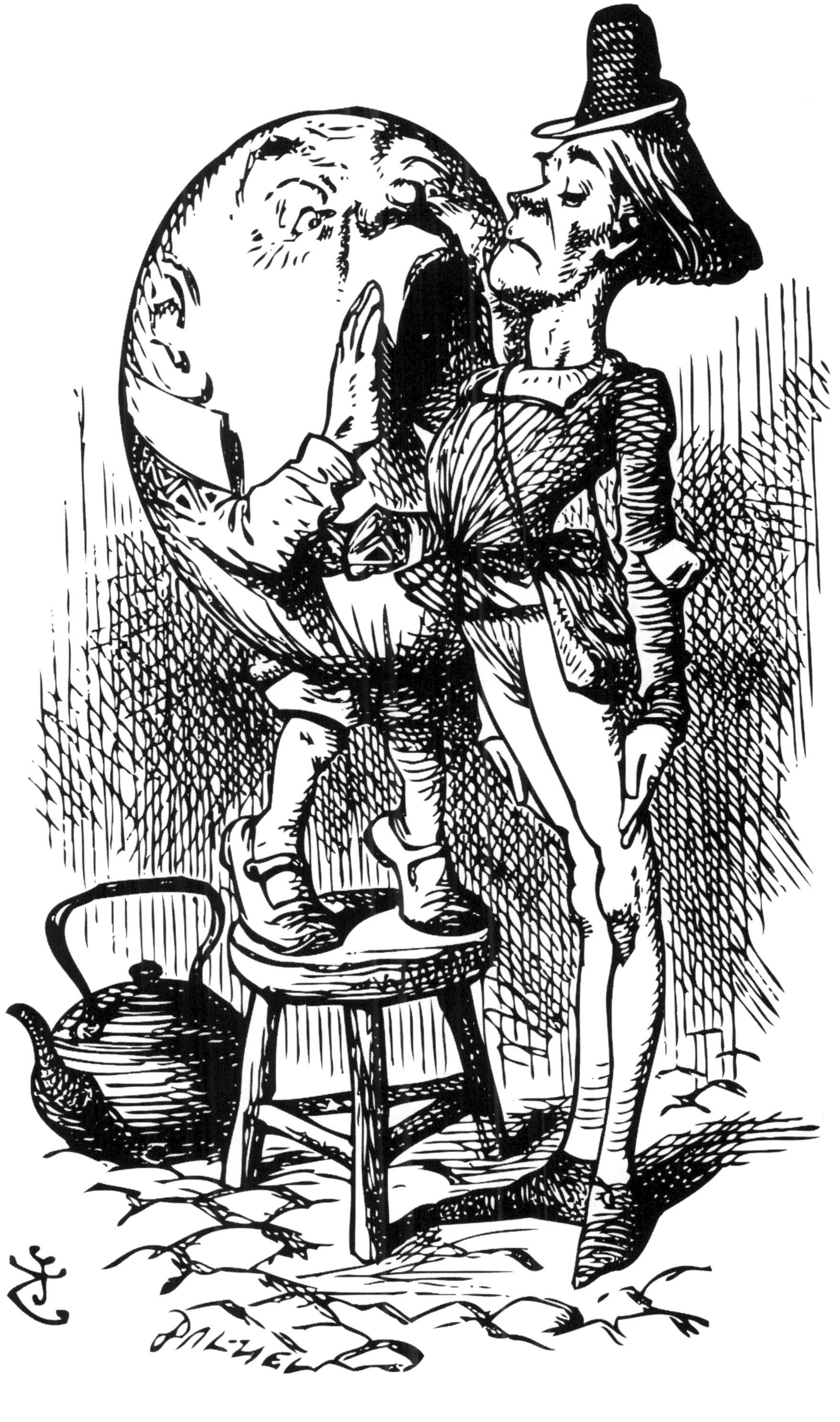

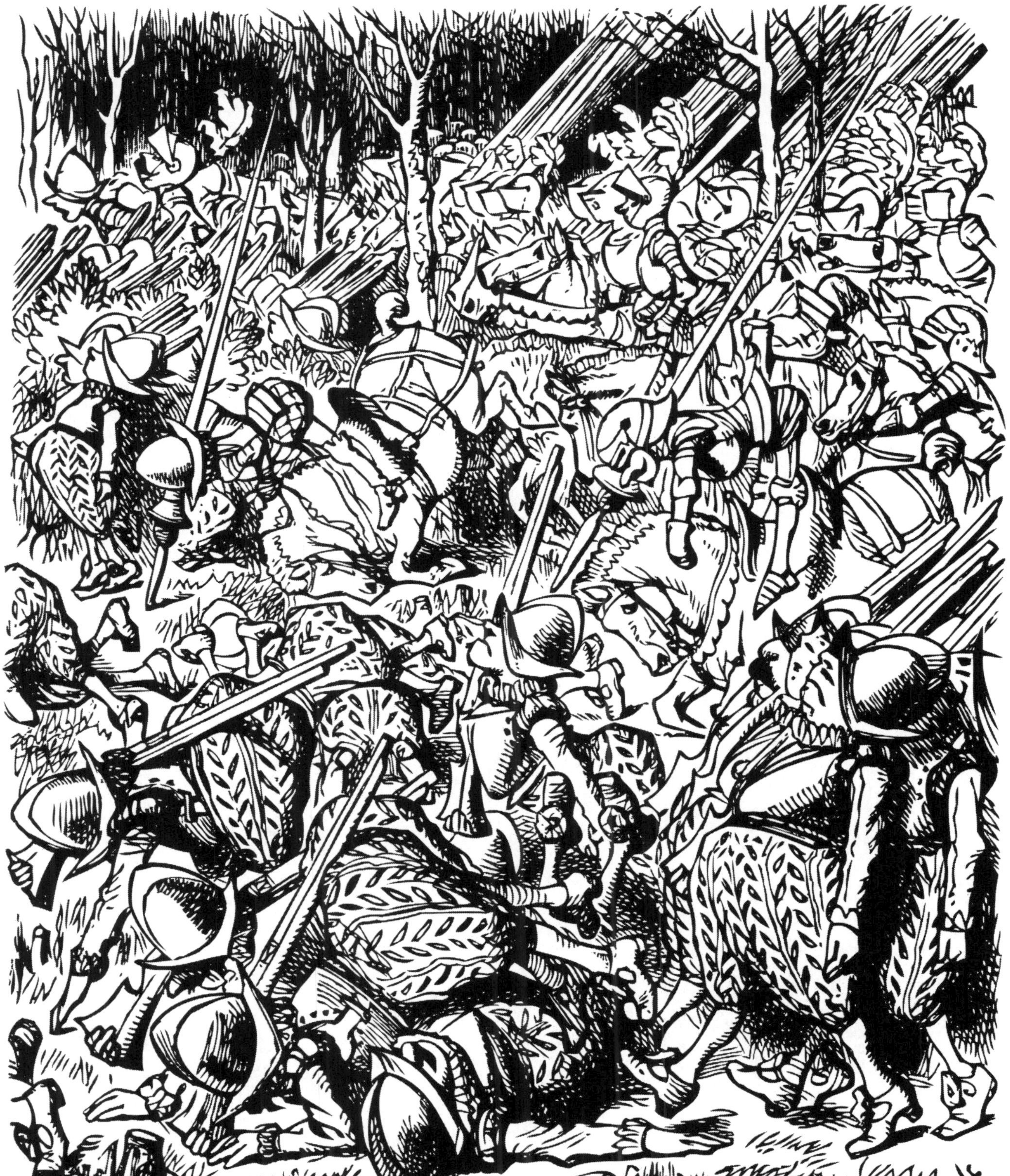

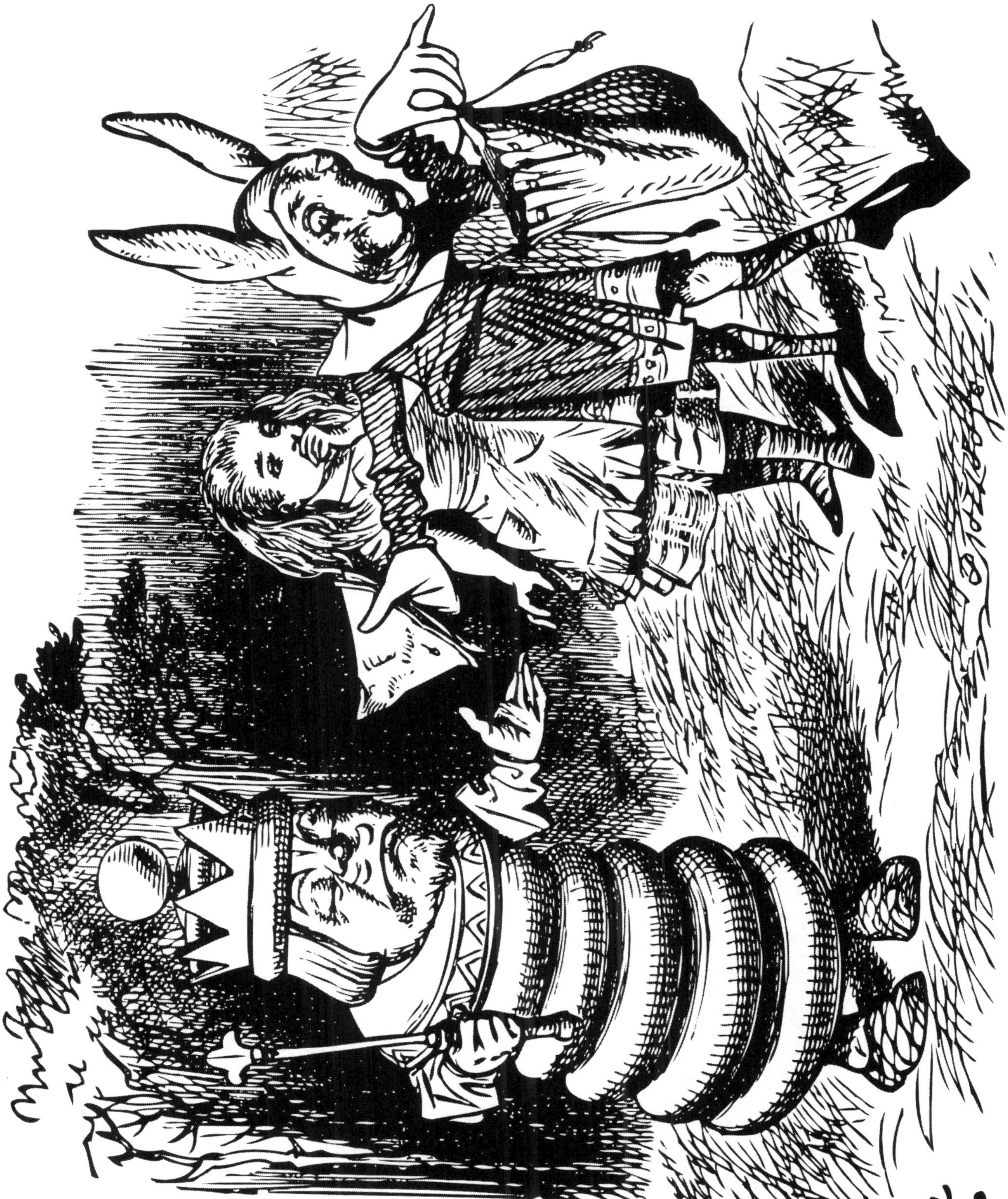

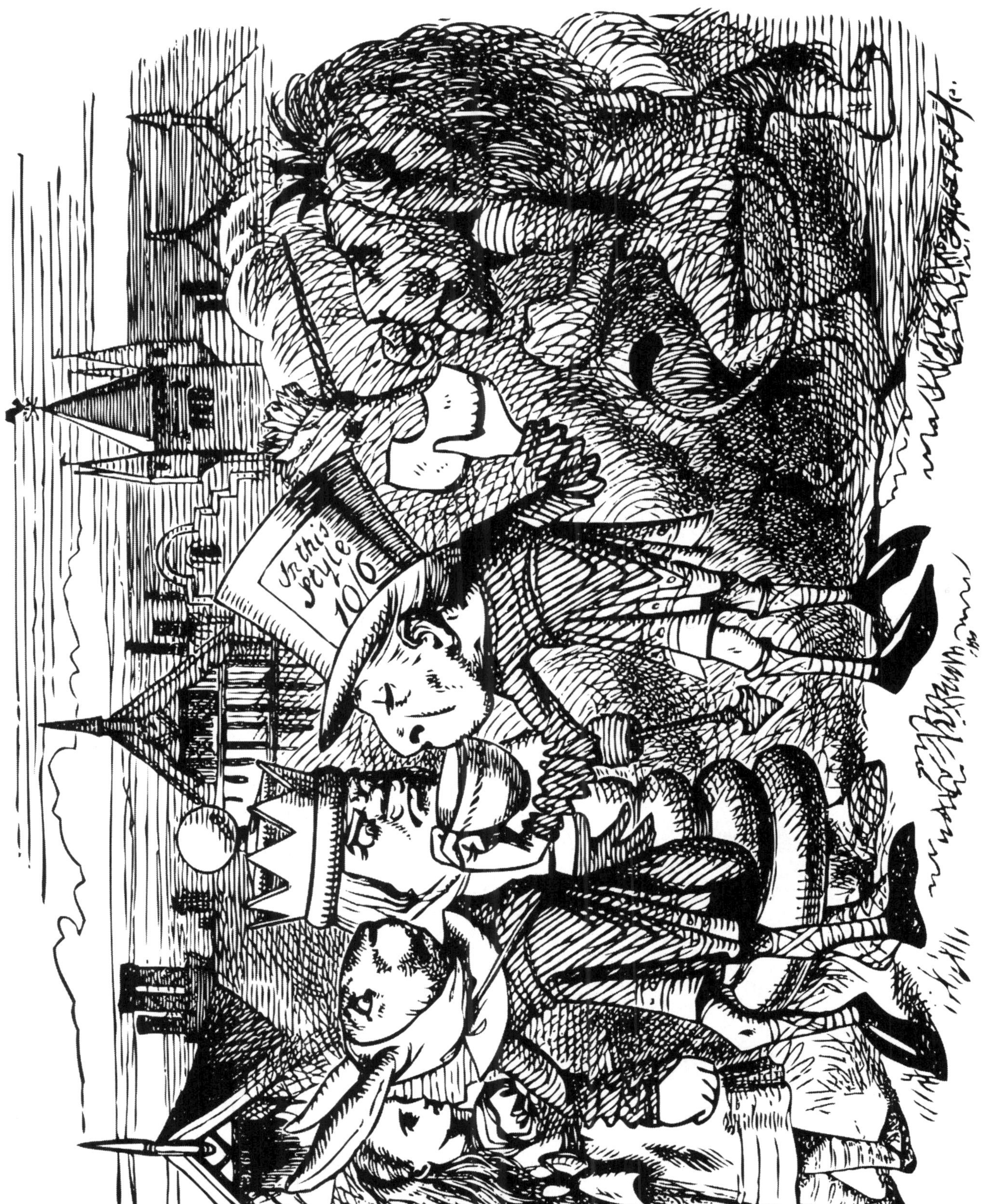
In this style 10/6

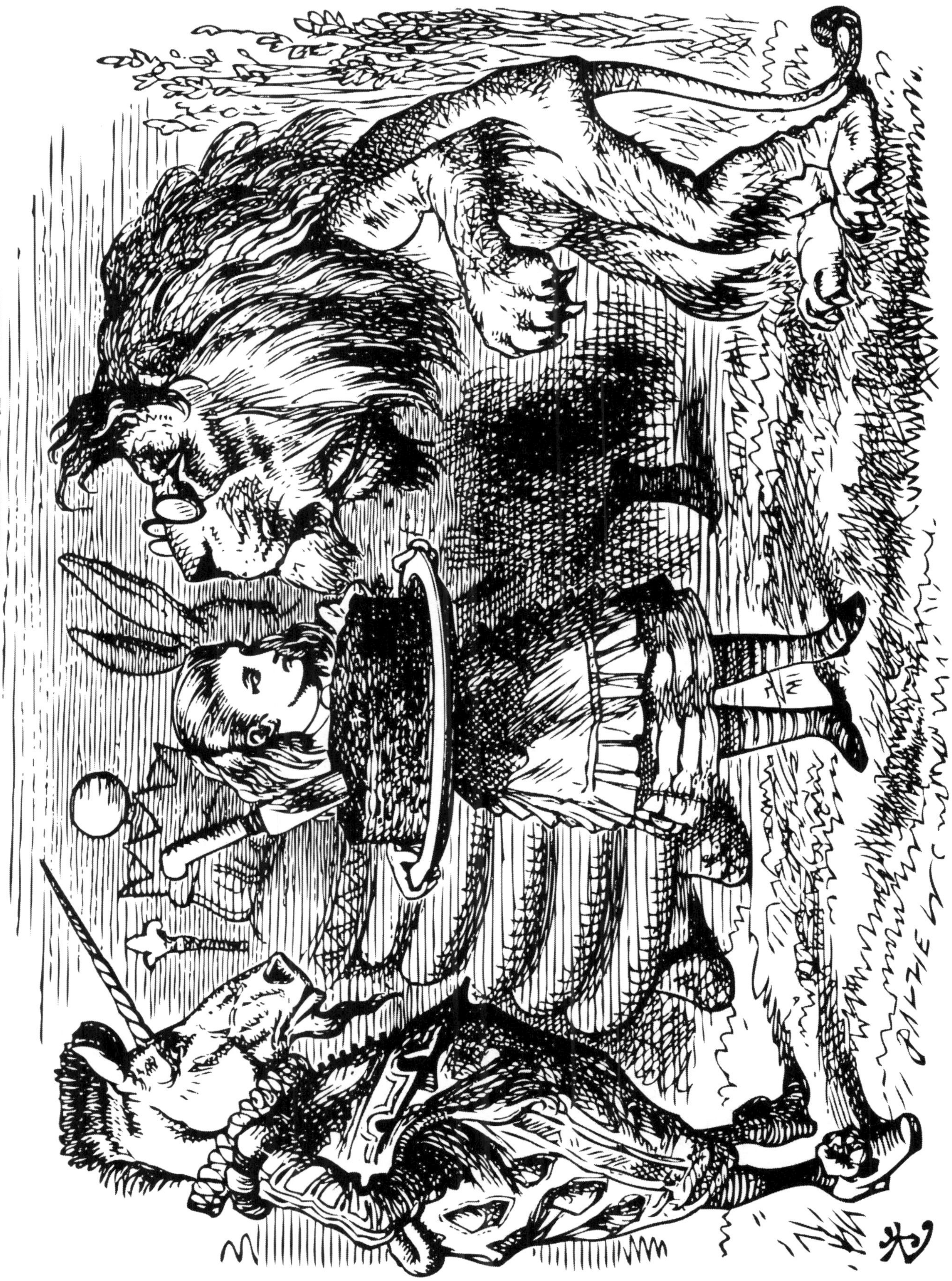

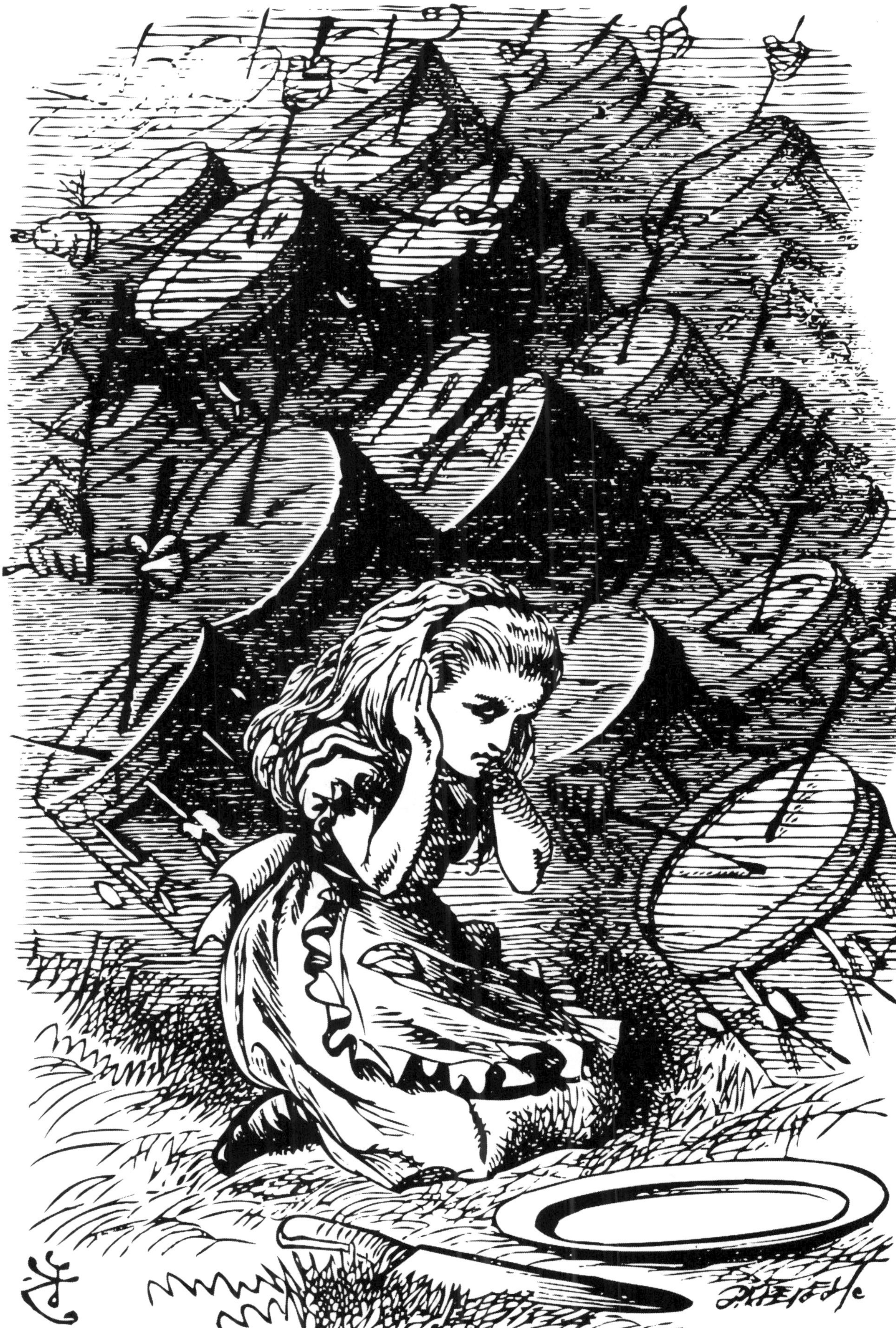

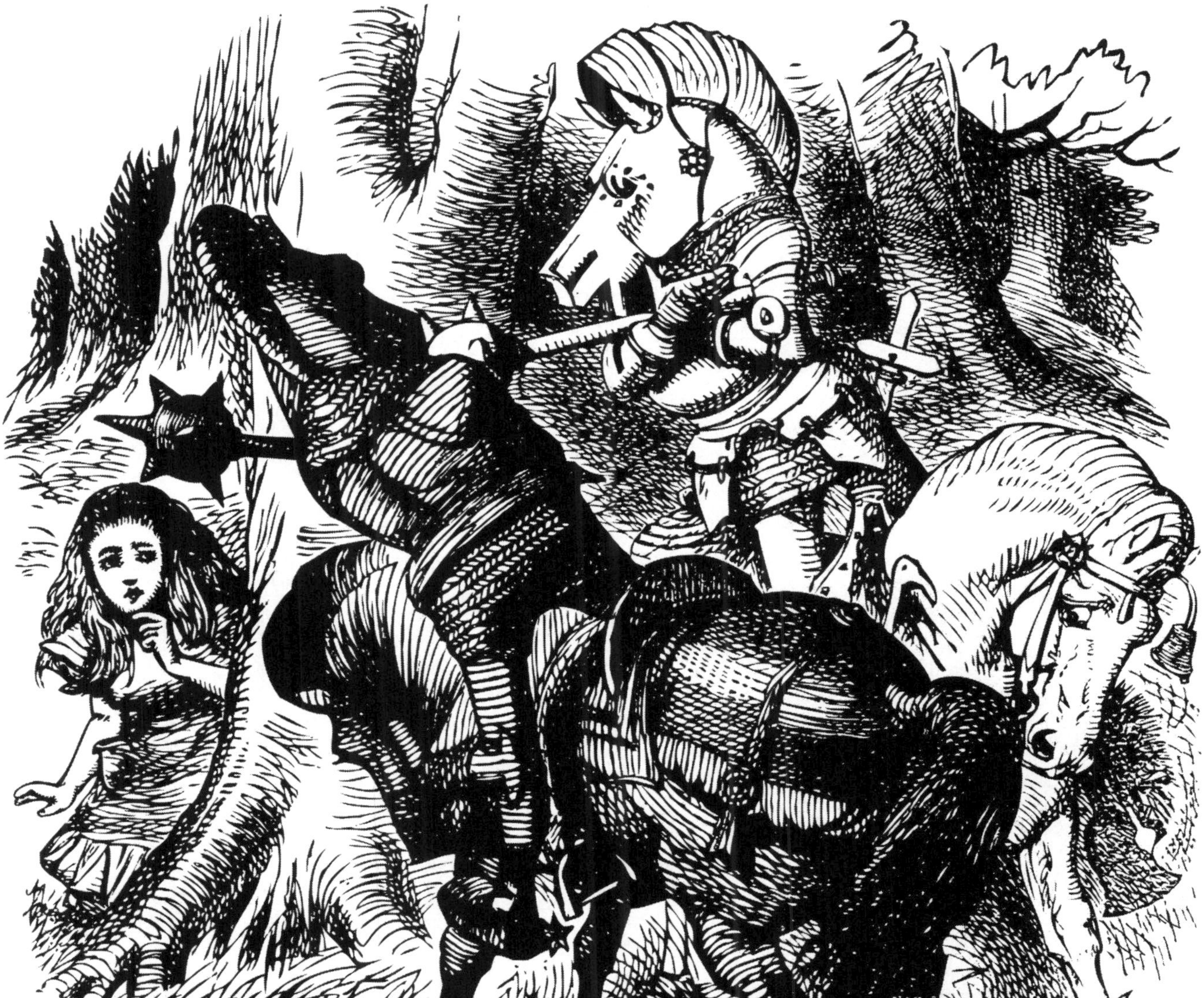

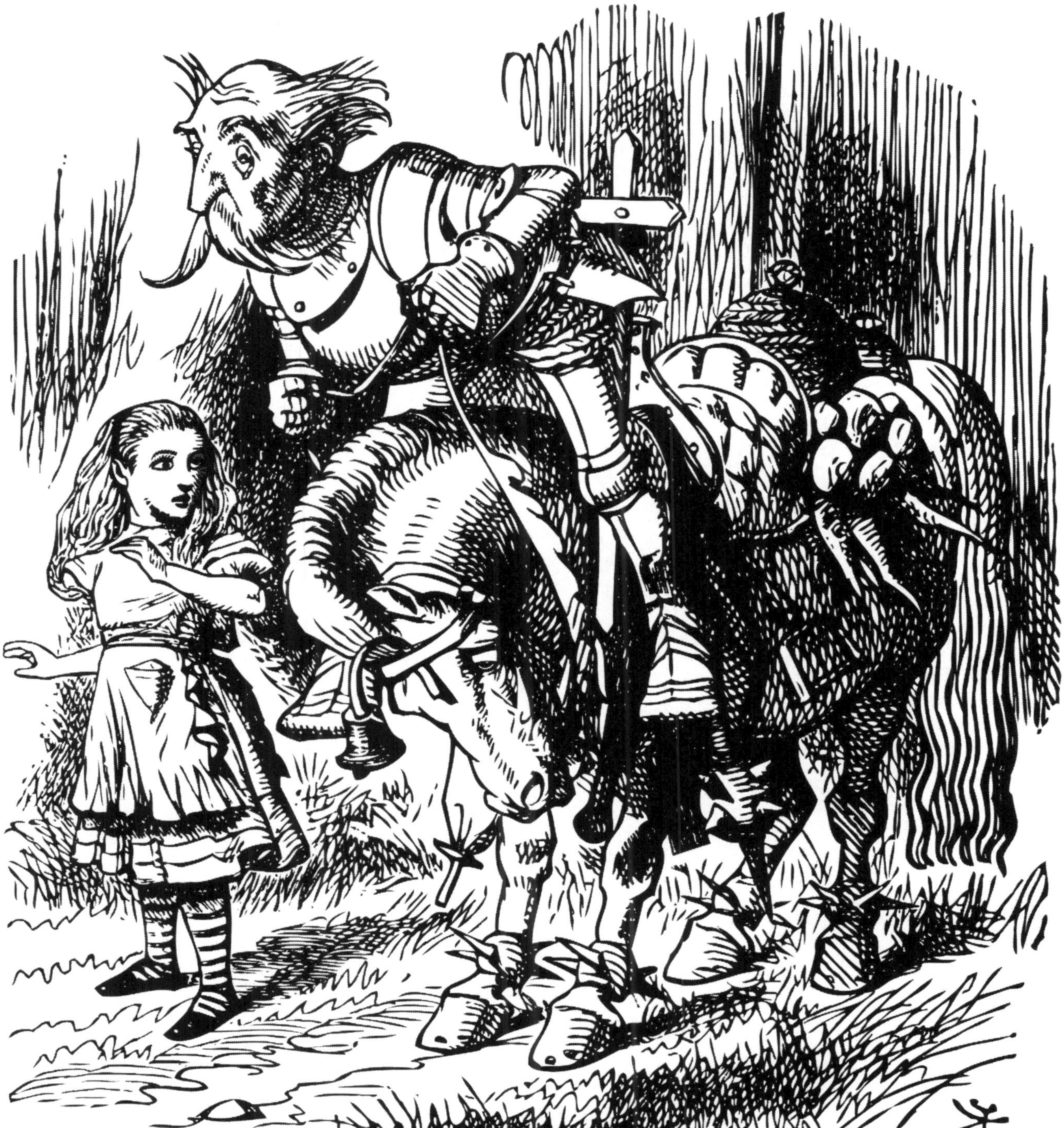

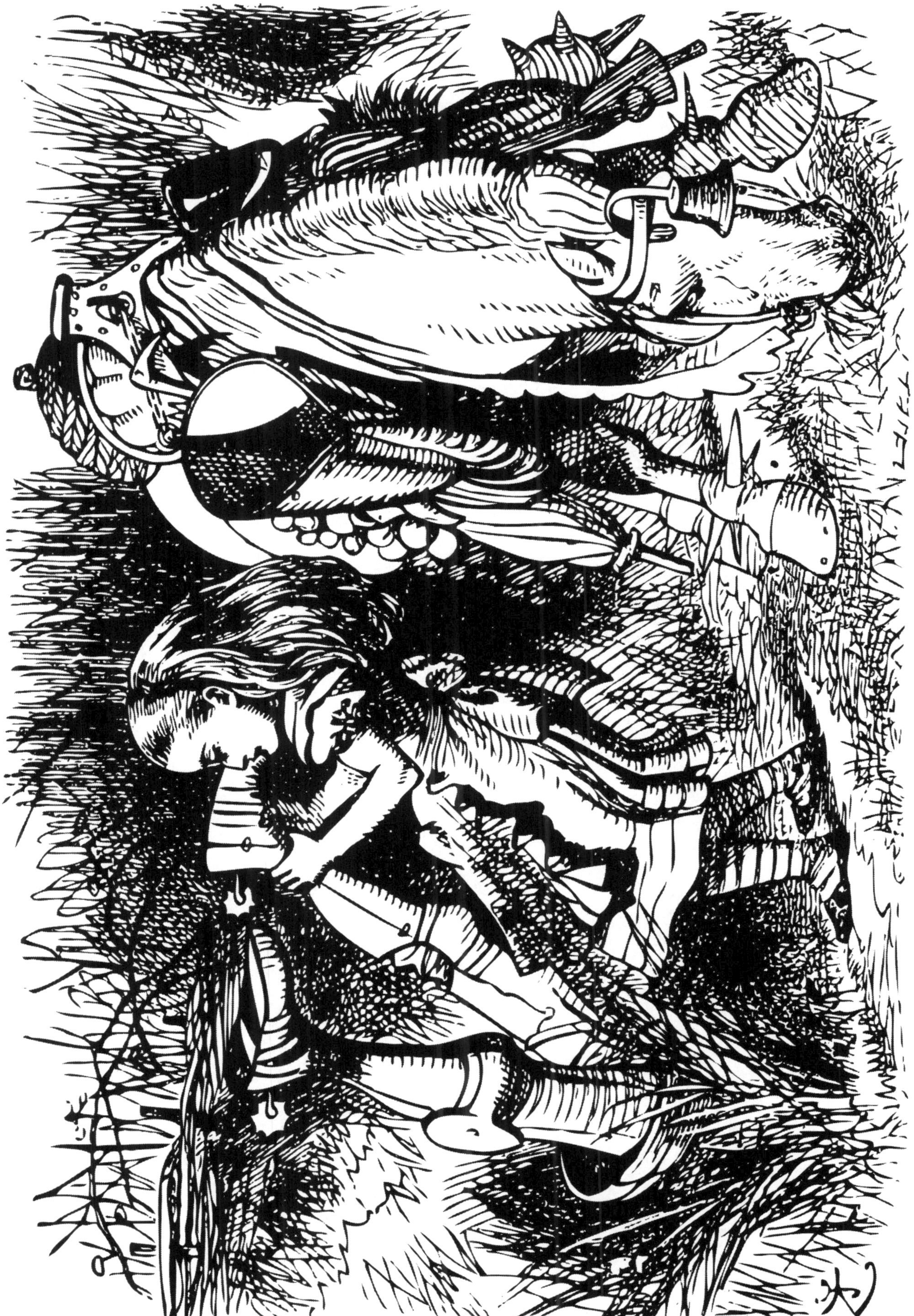

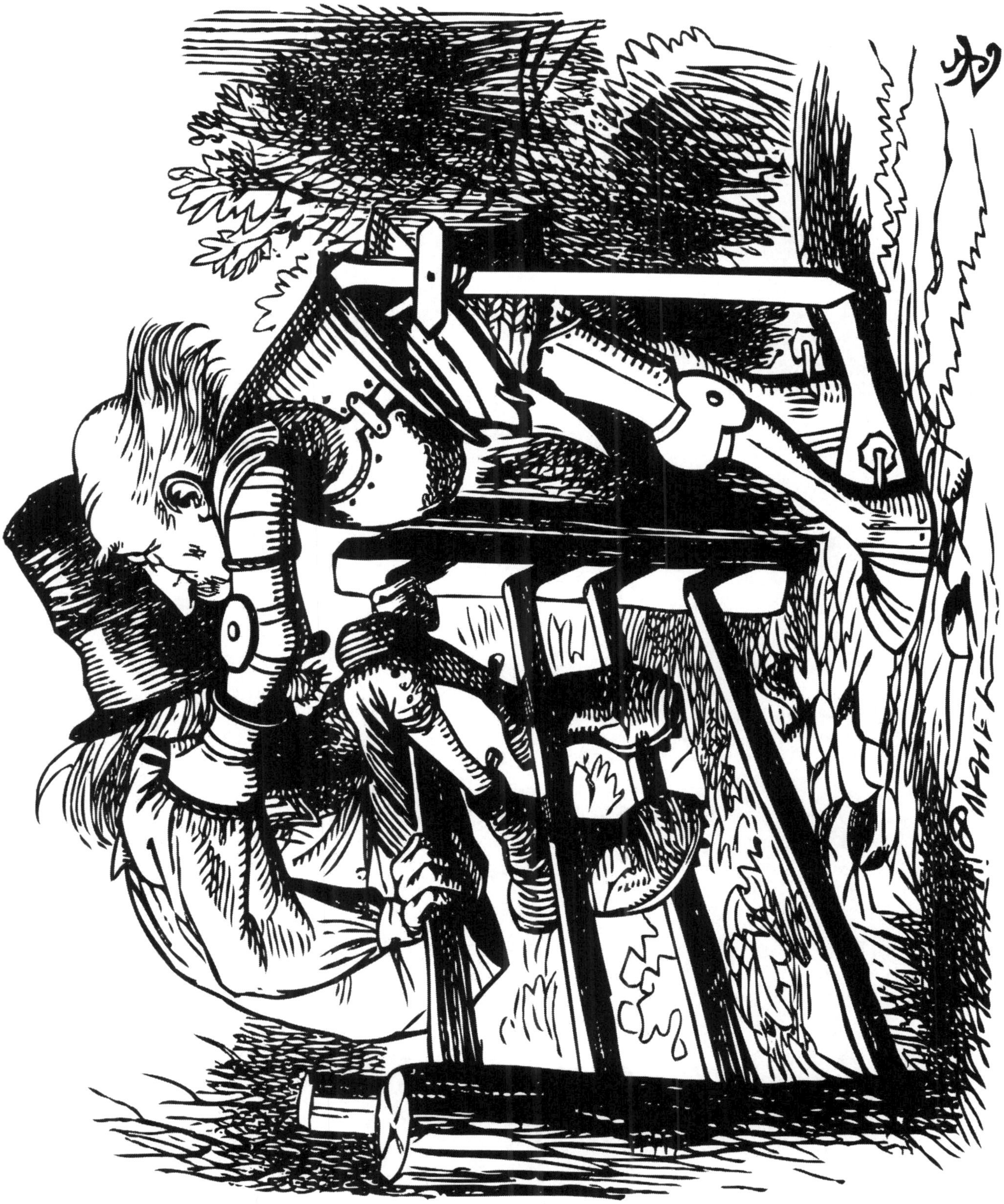

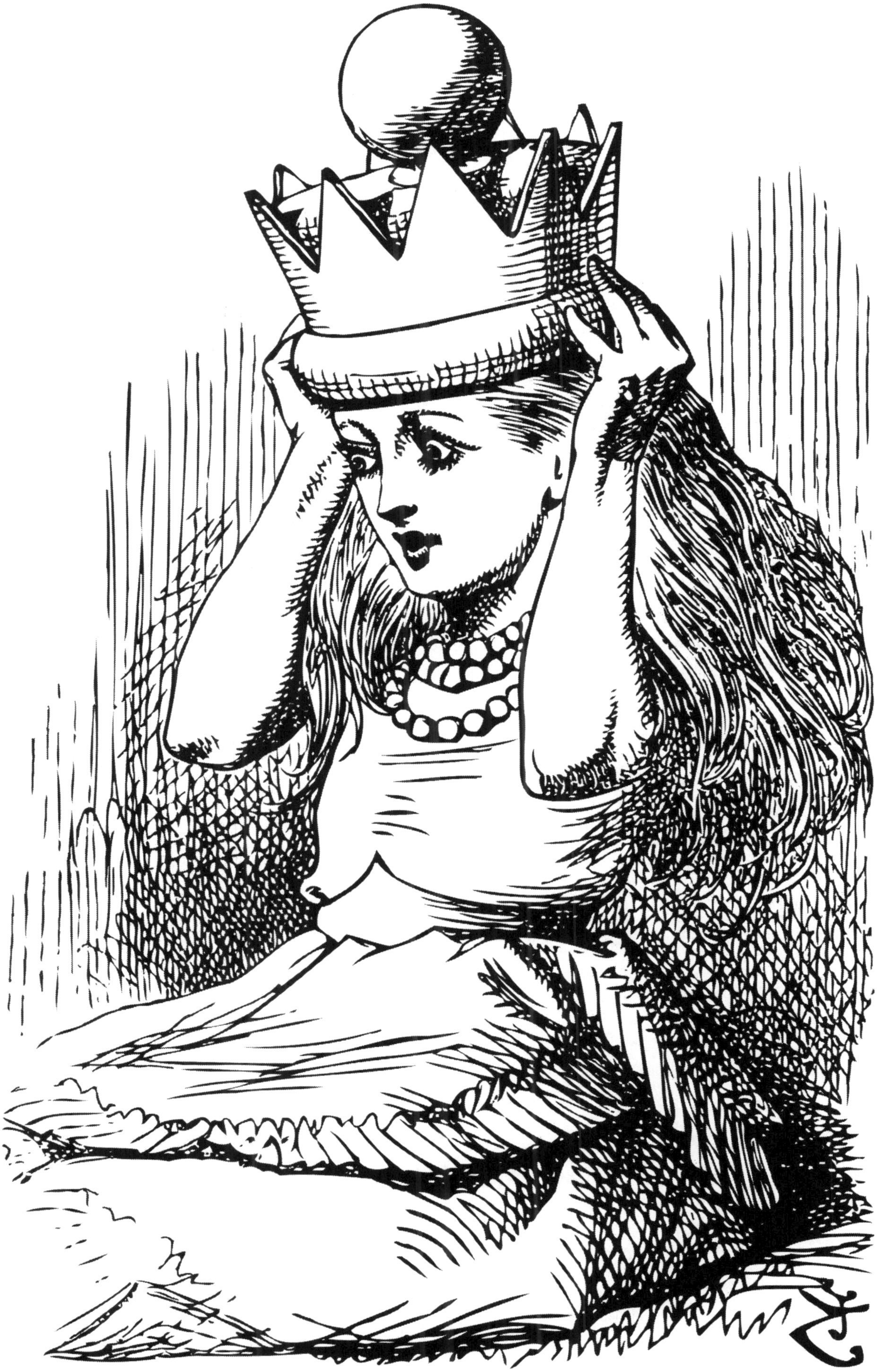

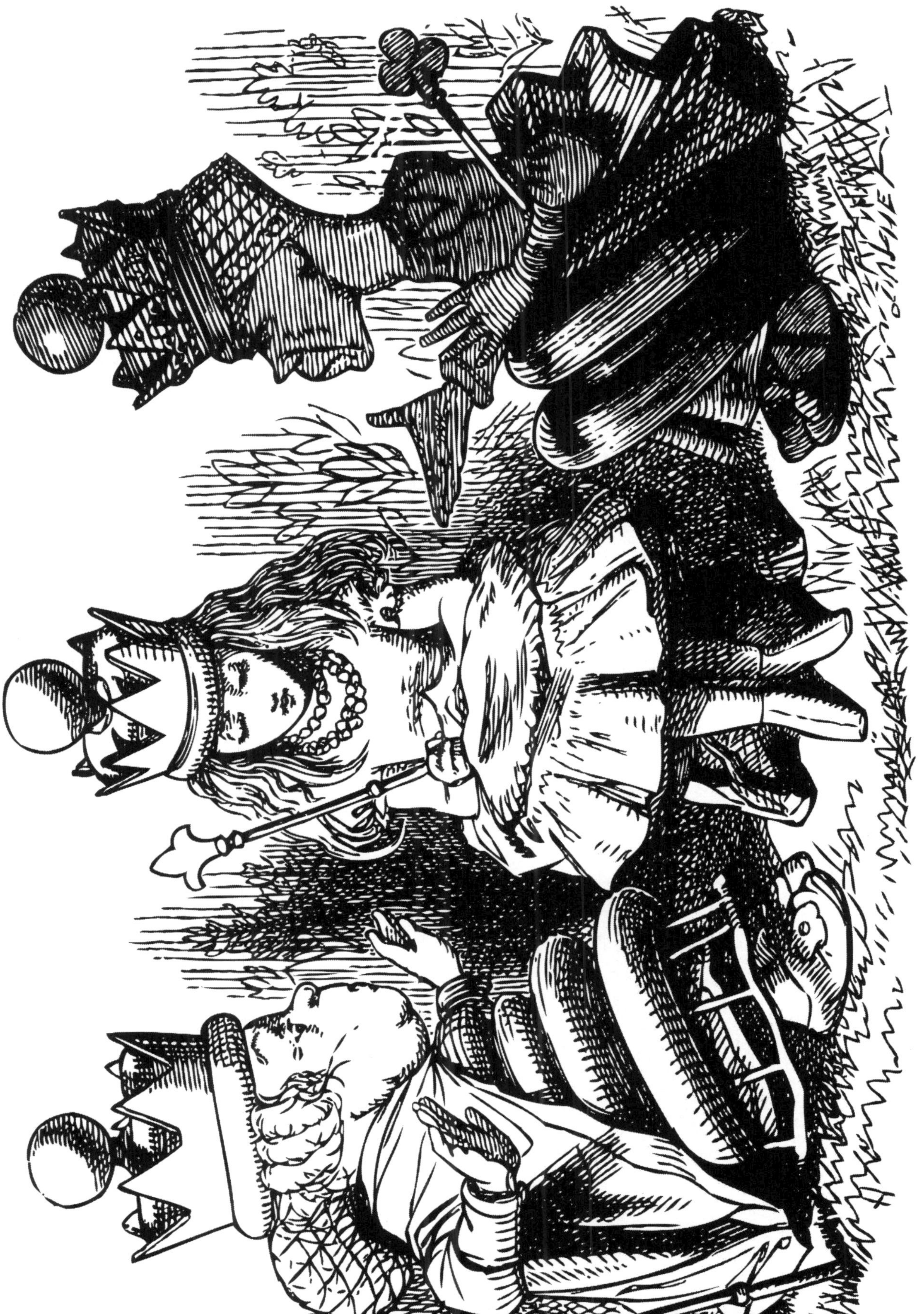

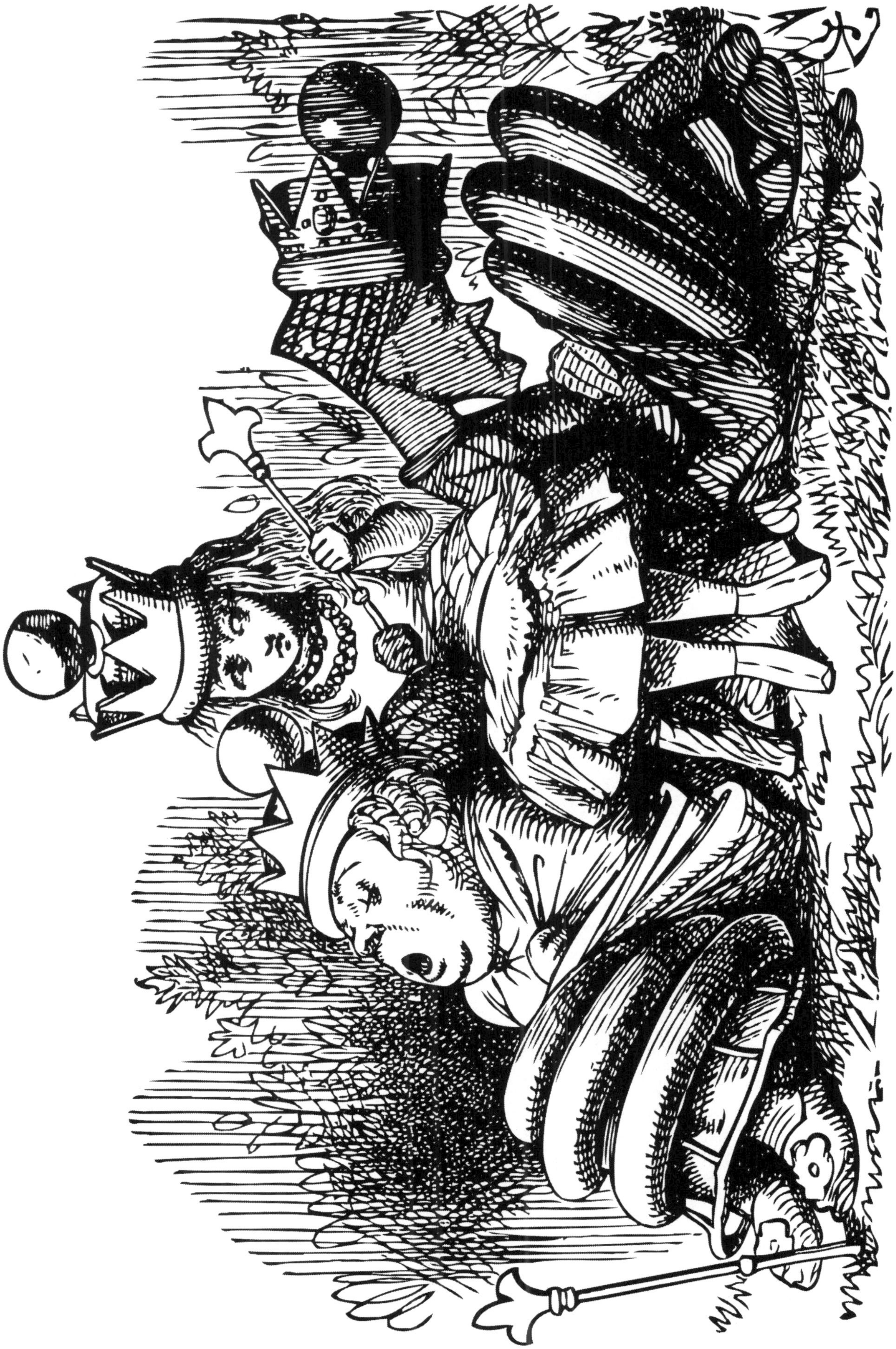

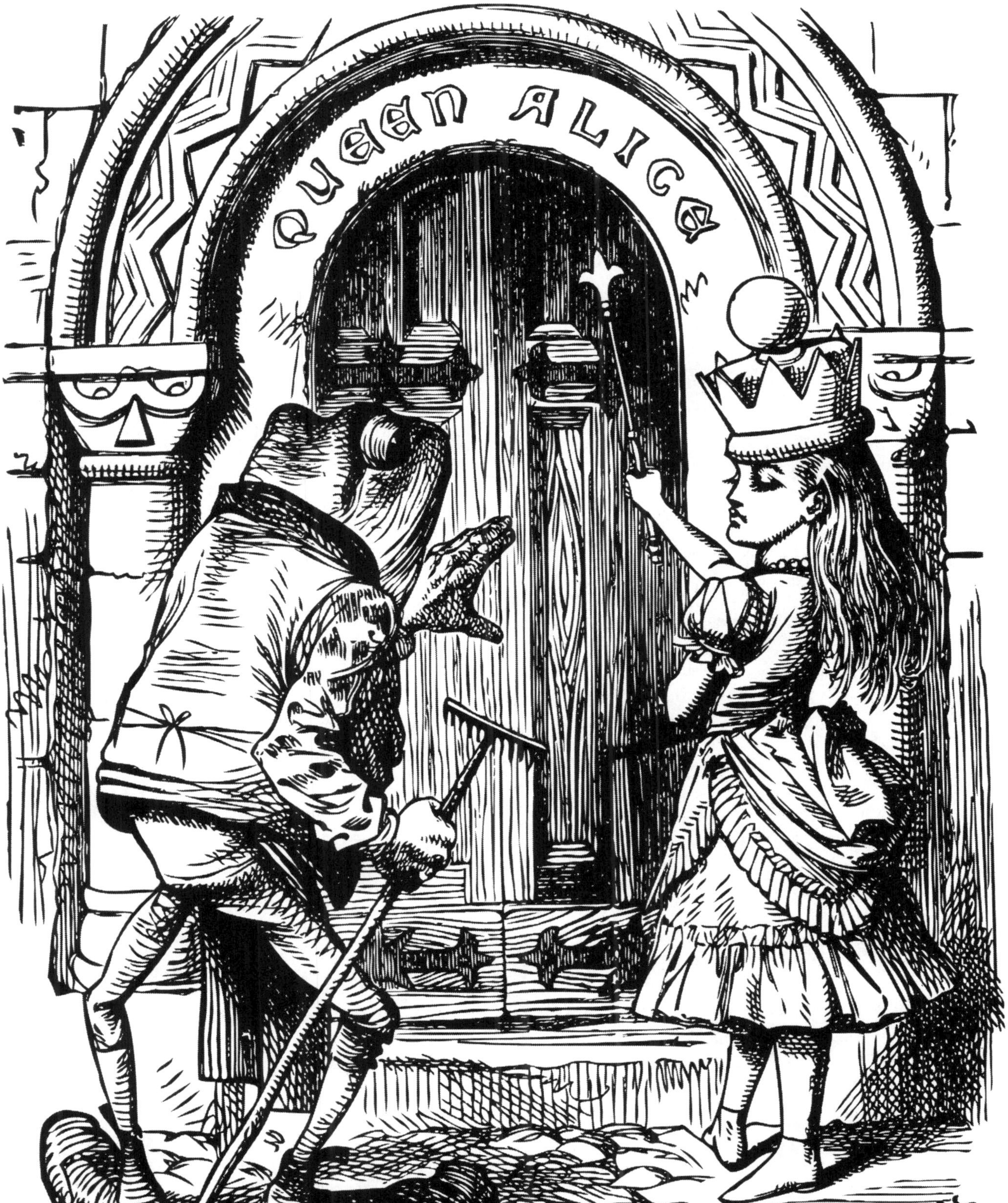
QUEEN ALICE

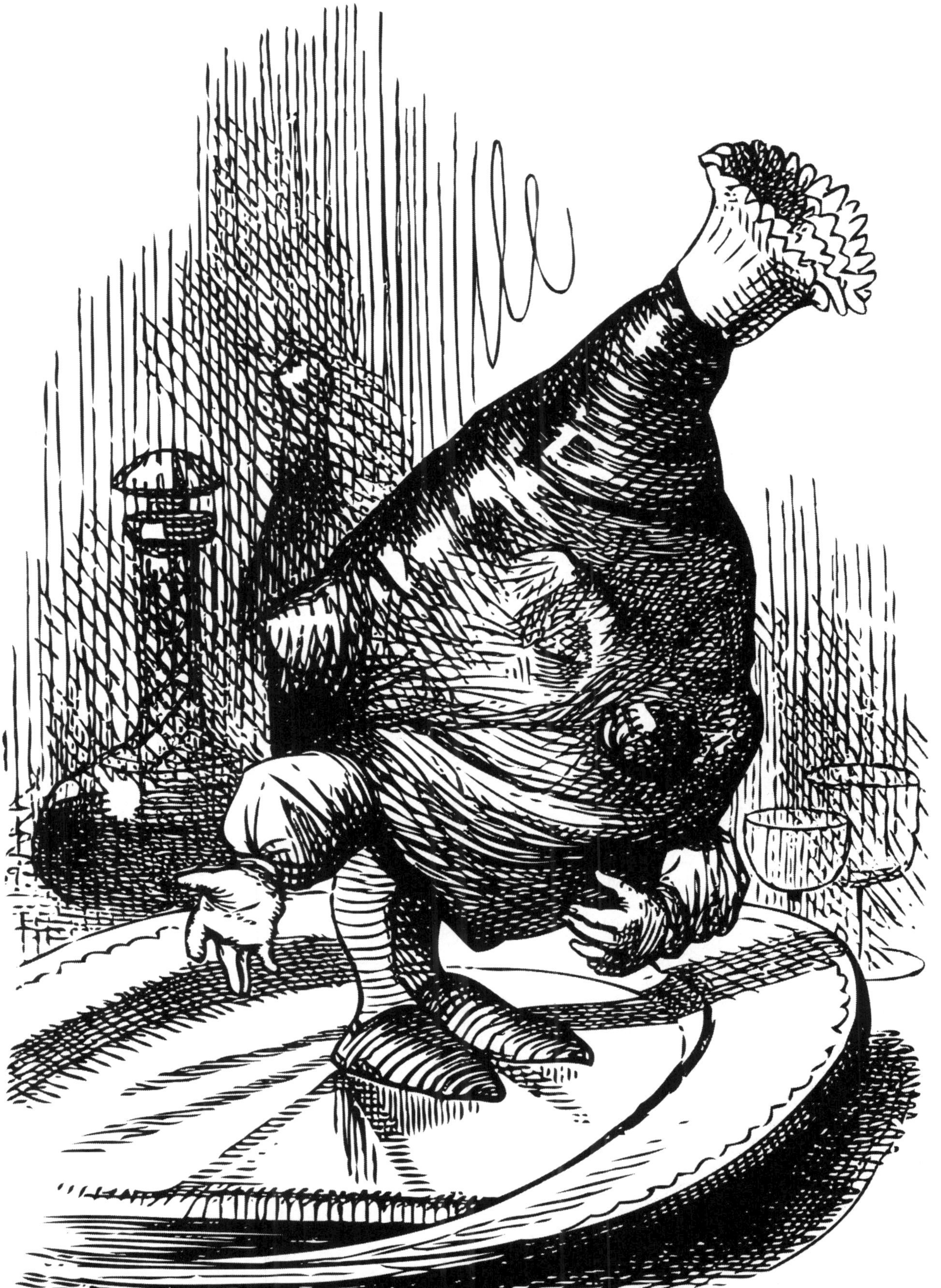

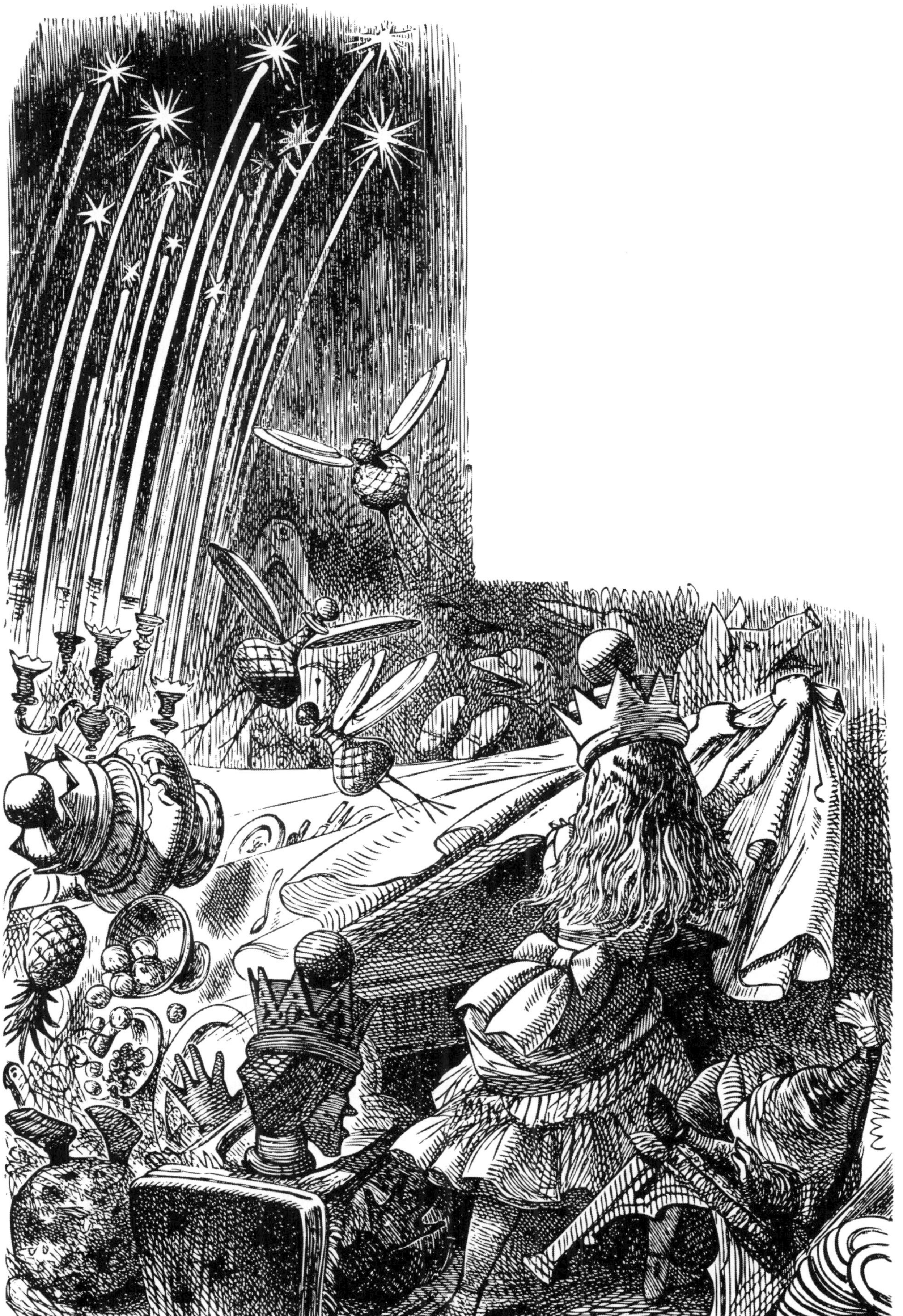

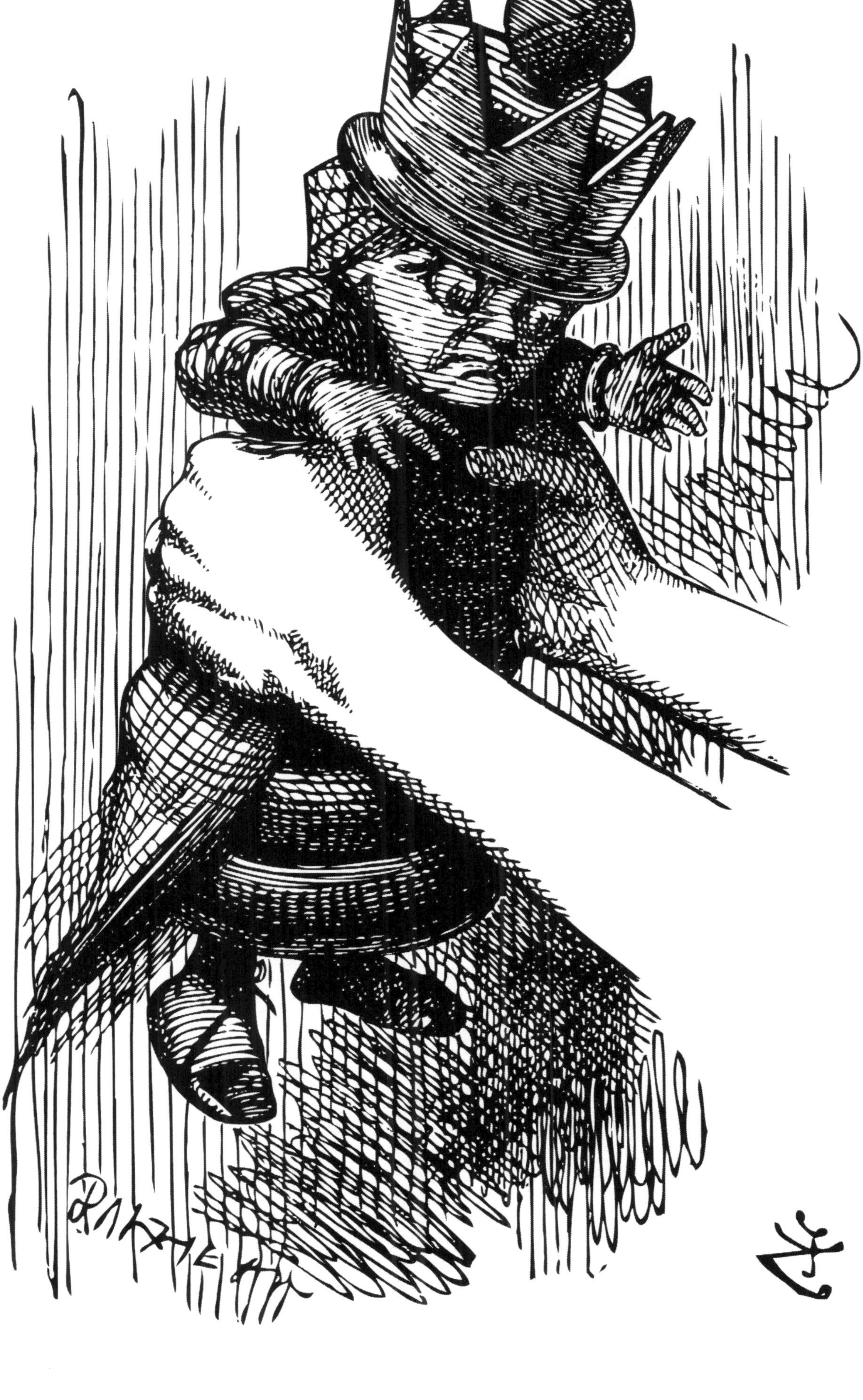

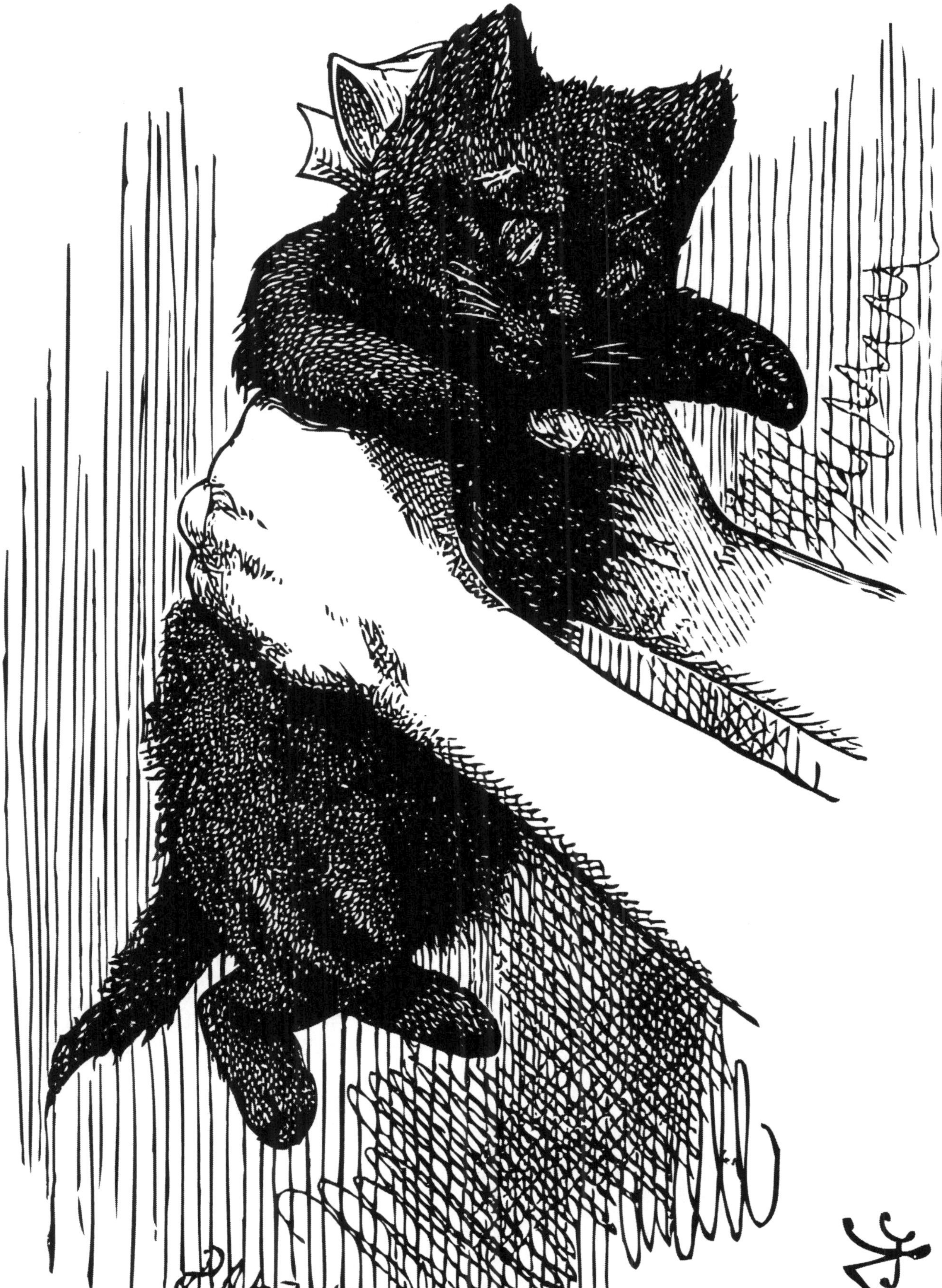

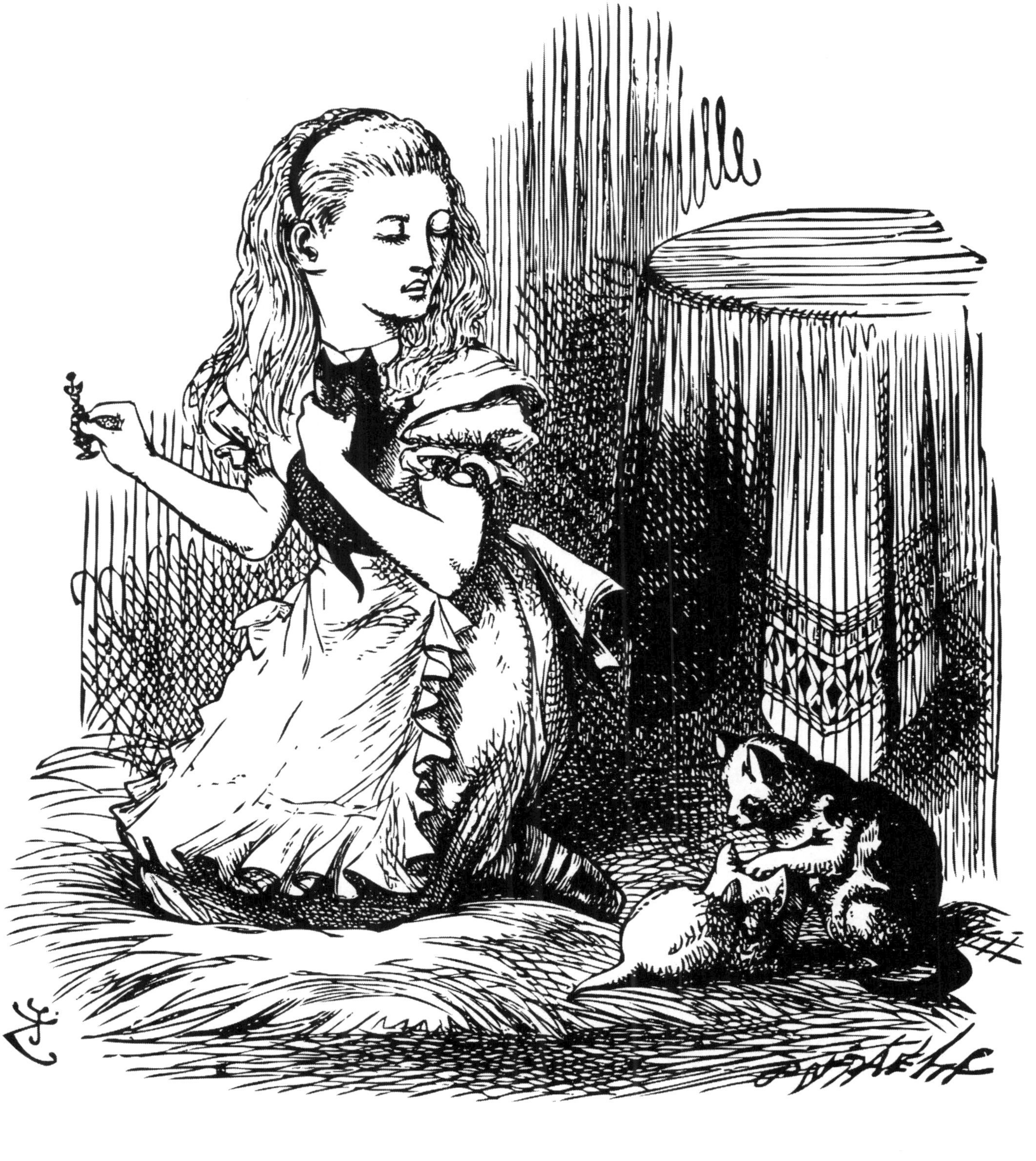

Manufactured by Amazon.ca
Bolton, ON

16212085R00061